EDUCATING AS AN ART

EDUCATING AS AN ART

Essays on Waldorf Education

REVISED EDITION,

CELEBRATING SEVENTY-FIVE

YEARS OF WALDORF EDUCATION

IN NORTH AMERICA

Edited by Carol Ann Bärtges and Nick Lyons

THE RUDOLF STEINER SCHOOL
NEW YORK CITY

Inquiries should be directed to:

The Rudolf Steiner School
15 East 79th Street
New York, NY 10021

Some of the articles in this book originally
appeared in the journal, *Education as an Art*.

Art Editors: Lucy Schneider and Rallou Malliarakis Hamshaw

Designed by Liz Driesbach

Photographs by Ellen Silverman

Editorial Assistant: Jena Davis Srivastava

Copy Editor: Jane Elias

Printed in Canada by Transcontinental Printing

Frontpiece: Twelfth grade artwork from the History
through Modern Art main lesson

CONTENTS

PART TWO: THE HIGH SCHOOL

EKKEHARD PIENING
November 19, 1941 – December 25, 1989

This seventy-fifth Anniversary edition of *Educating as an Art*
is dedicated in loving memory to Ekkehard Piening,
teacher and colleague at the Rudolf Steiner School

FOREWORD TO THE SEVENTY-FIFTH ANNIVERSARY EDITION

Coming to know the world must be on the wings of full engagement
— EKKEHARD PIENING (November 19, 1941–December 25, 1989)

Seventy-five years ago a group of five teachers prepared for the opening day of the first Rudolf Steiner School in America. All but one of these teachers had met with Rudolf Steiner and all had become deeply influenced by his spiritual-scientific teachings and his views on human development. On a crisp autumn morning in October 1928, twelve children of various ages came together in a New York City brownstone on East Thirty-seventh Street to meet their teachers and begin what would become the Waldorf education movement in this country. In addition to the school, the little brownstone housed the offices of Dr. Christoph Linder, father of our own woodwork teacher, Renate Poliakine, as well as the first headquarters of Weleda Incorporated, the international medical and pharmaceutical company. Every afternoon, chairs, desks, and school supplies were swept up and put away to make room for patients who consulted with Dr. Linder in the converted classrooms. Clearly, we in the New York City Rudolf Steiner School have a long history of learning to be flexible and accommodating in small spaces!

Twenty-five years ago the first edition of *Educating as an Art* was published in celebration of the Rudolf Steiner School's fiftieth birthday. The volume was the work and vision of two devoted individuals: the one, Ekkehard Piening, a longtime, beloved teacher in our school, the other, Nick Lyons, a parent with his wife, Mari, of four children who attended the school. In 1978, Ekkehard was teaching English and drama in our high school after completing eight years with the class of 1979. Ten years later, Ekkehard was to move to Hadley, Massachusetts, where he would found the now thriving Hartsbrook Waldorf School. A busy professor of English at Hunter College as well as founder of his own publishing company, Lyons Press, Nick was one of those parent volunteers whose expertise and commitment helped move the school forward in innumerable ways. The collaboration of these two gentlemen was hardly an accident, but a reflection of the unique partnership between teacher and parent that makes a Waldorf school such an enriching community. How fortunate we are that Nick Lyons,

Seventh grade watercolor painting

now a venerable alumni parent, agreed to cast his experienced editorial eye over the pages of this new edition of *Educating as an Art.*

In 2003, as we celebrate seventy-five years of Waldorf education in North America with the founding of the New York City Rudolf Steiner School, it seems appropriate, indeed vital, to bring to the larger school community the thoughts of those educators whose initiatives had such a profound impact not only on our school but on Waldorf education in general. Most of the original articles collected and edited by Ekkehard Piening and Nick Lyons twenty-five years ago are reprinted in this new edition. However, in keeping with the expansive spirit of the Waldorf School movement, which has influenced the creation of fledgling schools throughout the country with astonishing speed, we have included contributions from a new generation of teachers, among them many who currently work in New York, and others from Waldorf communities around the United States. Their articles reflect the important developments that have occurred in our technological age of the last twenty-five years, both in curriculum and in approaches to classroom teaching.

In the words of Ekkehard Piening in a taped interview shortly before his death in 1989, a Waldorf teacher is never a "purveyor of information," but a seeker, one who "strives to form a living relationship between teacher, student, and subject. In helping the students experience fully what they are learning, the teacher is a creator all over again and takes continual joy in that act of creation, no matter what his/her weakness may be." A meaningful engagement with the material allows the students, in turn, to become "co-creators, not mere spectators" in their own education. Parents and alumni who have experienced this kind of education firsthand will agree with the noted child psychologist Joseph Chilton Pearce, author of *Magical Child* and *The Crack in the Cosmic Egg*, who says, "If there is any one thing that the Waldorf system does, it is to nurture, protect, and develop beautifully the intelligence of the true child."

The events of September 11, 2001, have marked an irrevocable change in the biography of the United States. Its many resulting tragedies and consequences call for a collective change of consciousness around the world. We are in need of principled young people who will find new ways to respond to the global community, to our fragile ecosystem, to the very quality of human existence with moral certitude in their thoughts and deeds. In its relentless quest to meet the higher nature of each student, to address the invisible as well as the visible needs of the human being, Waldorf education can develop in young people the requisite capacities of compassion and initiative. The educators whose articles appear in this new edition of *Educating as an Art* represent the work of those thousands of teachers in North America who for seventy-five years have been challenged and exhilarated by the insights of Rudolf Steiner. This is a book about teaching written by teachers: those who, in the words of Ekkehard Piening, have brought the world to their students "on the wings of full engagement." We hope that their words will engage all those who treasure "educating as an art."

Carol Ann Bärtges '77
June 2003

PREFACE TO THE 1979 EDITION

Henry Barnes

In October 1928 a dozen children of varying ages came together with their new teachers in a New York City brownstone on East Thirty-eighth Street in Murray Hill, a few blocks south of Grand Central Station, and the Rudolf Steiner School began. Behind this modest beginning lay several years of preparatory work by a small but devoted group of teachers, parents, and friends who had come to recognize the need for an education that would nourish the spiritual and artistic sides of a child's nature, as well as school his intellect and train his technical skills. Following highly individual paths, they had each at some point discovered in Rudolf Steiner's work a modern, scientific approach to an understanding of the human being and his place in the world and had come to see in this worldview a source for educational renewal. They were aware of the foundation by Rudolf Steiner in 1919 of the Waldorf School in Stuttgart, which had rapidly grown to be the largest nondenominational independent school in Germany, and of the sister schools that had been established in Holland, Switzerland, Germany, and England. That a similar school should exist in New York City had become their cherished ideal.

Now, fifty years later, the Rudolf Steiner School takes its place among the independent schools in New York City, educating boys and girls from kindergarten through to college.

What stood behind the foundation of the Rudolf Steiner School in New York City fifty years ago? What stands being the growing Waldorf educational movement in North America today?

Behind the establishment of the Rudolf Steiner School, New York, in 1928, were nine years of pioneer educational effort in Germany, Switzerland, Holland, Britain, and the Scandinavian countries. Farsighted teachers, parents, and social leaders had seen that World War I marked the beginning of the end of Western civilization in the one-sidedly materialistic, technological form that had become dominant during the course of the nineteenth century. Only a renewal, they realized, that sprang from its very source could give Western culture the new direction it needed. Turning the clock back would not help. Cultural renewal must be based on a science that could penetrate to the wellsprings of human nature, showing man how he could evolve a consciousness capable of attaining knowledge of spiritual as well as material realities. And for such a renewal, a new education was needed—an education in keeping with the demands of the times.

It was out of this recognition that Emil Molt, owner of the Waldorf-Astoria cigarette factory in Stuttgart, approached Rudolf Steiner immediately after the close of the war and asked him to establish a school for the children of the workers in his factory. Steiner replied that he would do so on the condition that the school be open to children of all social, economic, racial, and religious backgrounds; that it should be a unified twelve-year curriculum, cutting across the traditional European division whereby the academically oriented were separated out from the rest of the school population at the age of eleven plus; and that the school should be entirely free to develop its educational policies and methods and to place its administration in the hands of those who carried the day-to-day educational responsibility, namely its teachers. It was self-understood that Rudolf Steiner would be a member of the faculty and the school's first director.

Within a few years the Freie Waldorfschule, Stuttgart, had more than a thousand students, and before Steiner's death in 1925 similar schools had been established in Switzerland, Holland, and Germany and a school was in process of establishment in England. The Nationalist Socialist government that came to power in Germany in 1933 immediately set about undermining and destroying the Waldorf schools, as well as all of Steiner's work. It was publicly stated that there could not be a system of schools within a National-Socialist state that had as its expressed goal the education of children and young people to think for themselves. After five years of slow strangulation, the Stuttgart school was finally closed by the Hitler government in 1938, immediately following the annexation of Austria. The rebirth of the Waldorf schools in Germany and Holland after the war was dramatic. The Stuttgart school was the very first to reopen in Baden-Wurtemberg; former teachers, parents, and students appeared from nowhere to help clear the rubble, working at first with their bare hands in near-starvation condition. The Allied Military Government gave the reopening of the Waldorf schools every support, recognizing in them the seeds of a free cultural life and a democratic citizenry. Former schools reopened, new ones were founded, and by 1960 there were 25 Waldorf schools in Western Germany, although not one behind the Iron Curtain. There are 150 recognized Waldorf schools throughout the world, making the Waldorf School Movement in all probability the largest nonsectarian, independent elementary and secondary school movement in the world.*

* Editor's note: Today there are over one thousand Waldorf schools worldwide.

Yet for us in the United States, the proliferation of Waldorf schools and the strength of this educational movement, especially in Europe since World War II, is something of a riddle. How is it that Waldorf education is virtually unknown in this country? There is surely no school of education in which reference is not made to Montessori or Froebel, or to the work of Piaget, yet Steiner is rarely mentioned and the existence of a widespread and well-established school movement drawing on his insights is a source of astonishment even to the well informed. This situation is indeed changing, but the fact that it has prevailed for the past fifty years and has continued almost unabated up to the present day points to a fundamental aspect of Steiner's work and, with it, of Waldorf education.

In a world that prizes the quantity of facts and the speed of their assimilation, certain vital qualities of a child's growth easily go unnoticed. What characterizes Waldorf education is not primarily its content, although this may be interesting and innovative, but the spirit out of which the curriculum and methods grow. A teacher in a Steiner or Waldorf school strives to learn to "read" something of the children's true nature from the way in which they appear to his observation. How they speak and walk and use their hands is as interesting to him as how they form their thoughts. How they paint, draw, model, do sums, listen to a story or to instructions, how they play and apply themselves, how they relate to their peers and to those younger or older than themselves, or to those in trouble, these are all letters in a living alphabet through which the teacher tries to read answers to the question: who are these children in their deeper being? Every musician must learn to master his instrument and each human being has gradually to take possession of the bodily instrument that he inherits. He has to learn to absorb, to adjust to, and transform the influences coming from his environment, little by little making this physical and cultural instrument his own, setting his individual stamp upon it so that through it, and with it, he can make that "music" for which he was born.

This musician, the human individuality, is not only a citizen of the world we know through our senses. He is a being of soul and spirit, living according to inner laws but manifesting in the physical world. The educator—parent, teacher, or friend—has the task of so working with the bodily organism, with the habits, with the characteristic qualities of individuality that seeks to come to expression through them. Over the individuality itself we have no control, nor the right even to wish to control it. We have but to try to recognize it, to respect, protect, and encourage it. Our work as educators in the broadest sense is to further its inherent development, to free it from encumbrances, to challenge and stimulate, but also to offer the resistance that it needs in order to grow independent and inwardly sturdy and strong. Our task is to work with the instrument, to balance and heal it, to curb its excesses, and to strengthen its weaknesses so that, in its own time, the individuality can emerge, ready and able to take charge of its own self-direction and self-discipline—the charioteer who can guide the steeds of his own emotional and mental nature toward the goals that he has freely chosen.

This, in broad strokes, is the picture of man that stands behind Waldorf or Steiner education: a being of soul and spirit as well as body, subject to psychic and spiritual laws as well as to the laws that govern his physical and biological environment. But a being who develops according to predictable stages that can be recognized and understood as exactly as the stages of physical development.

On what authority does this knowledge of man rest? On the same authority upon which all knowledge must rest today—that of an objective, disciplined scientific approach to experience; only in the case of Steiner's work this approach has been extended beyond the limits of sense perception to knowledge of the supersensible. Steiner's immense life-work, which is bearing practical fruits in fields as disparate as medicine, agriculture, mathematics, education, and the arts, does not ask to be believed but to be tested and understood. Its claim to be accepted as knowledge, not faith, is based on the methods by which its results are achieved. What constitutes science's claim to objectivity is not its *content* but its *method*, a method that must at all times be conscious, controlled, and reproducible. An investigation of spiritual phenomena that is conducted according to clear laws of scientific procedure has the same claim to validity as the investigation of physical phenomena that can be counted, weighed, and measured. But there is one important difference. In the material sciences, criteria are quantifiable, they yield to statistical treatment. A subjective observer who exercises his own judgment is more and more ruled out. So-called objective, usually technological, procedures take over. In spiritual science, however, this is not the case. Here the conscious, self-critical human being is himself the instrument of observation and must, therefore, raise his soul to a level of objectivity at which every step is transparent and subject to the same controls as in every other scientific procedure. Above all, the methods of spiritual investigation claiming to be scientific must be capable of reproduction so that any other investigator who prepares himself in the same way and follows the same procedures will arrive at the same results. In each of his basic cognitive works, which include *The Philosophy of Spiritual Activity, Knowledge of the Higher Worlds and Its Attainment, Theosophy,* and *Occult Science: an Outline,* as well as in countless lectures, Rudolf Steiner describes the path of knowledge pursued in obtaining the results and explains how every unprejudiced thinker and observer can educate himself to be able to come to the same insight.

It is out of this background of spiritual-scientific investigation that the knowledge of man upon which Waldorf education is built has been achieved. Although the method of investigation is comparable to that of material science on which every education, including that offered in religious schools, is based, the results of spiritual-scientific investigation often differ radically from what is traditionally acceptable today. They describe man from the spiritual and psychic as well as from the physical point of view and place him in relation with a world totality that sees nonphysical causes at work within the world that we normally experience. However, the careful work of disciplined observers like Piaget, Gesell, Raymond Moore, and many others corroborates the findings of spiritual-scientific research. As Steiner's work comes to be known as an objective contribution to the knowledge of man and of pedagogical methods, it will receive the recognition it deserves. Only then can it unfold the health-giving influence in American education of which it so eminently capable.

It is from this point of view that this volume of essays is offered to the general reader. It does not pretend to be systematic or exhaustive, but each article describes a facet of life and work in a Rudolf Steiner school, and it is hoped that together they will form a mosaic of experience and thus serve to commemorate the first fifty years of pioneer enterprise in this educational field.

EDUCATION AS AN ART
The Rudolf Steiner Method

Henry Barnes and Nick Lyons

The heart of the Steiner method is the belief that education is an art. Whether the subject is arithmetic or history or physics, the presentation must live—it must speak to the child's experience. To educate the whole child, his heart and will must be reached, as well as his mind.

First, in the Rudolf Steiner or Waldorf method, comes the *encounter*; then encounter becomes *experience*; and out of experience the *concept* crystallizes. Encounter, experience, concept—perception, feeling, idea: these are the three steps in every genuine learning process.

For instance, the fourth-grader at a Steiner school studies the animals in their relation to man. He encounters the cuttlefish. This creature lurks beneath a stone on the ocean floor, its eight tentacles weaving in the moving currents. Its body is all head. Senses alert, it waits to seize its passing prey.

The facts are presented in graphic detail as pure observation, vivid to the lively inner eye of a nine-year-old's imagination. The encounter is direct perception, the child's will is engaged, and he lives in the scene as he would if he were absorbed in a play at the theater. When the presentation is completed, the teacher reminds the children of what they have heard and seen about this strange sea creature. How like the head of man it is, with its bony skull, its active sense, even its protective cloud of squirted ink like a small boy's cloud of words to hide in! The children recall the vivid first impressions with feelings of astonishment, revulsion, curiosity. The encounter becomes experience as feelings unite with perceptions.

Full of the cuttlefish, the children go to other classes, then home, and finally to bed. The experience is "slept over" and then they return to school in the morning, awaiting the last act of the drama. "What makes the cuttlefish so different from a regular fish— a bluefish or a mackerel? They both live in the water?" The teacher's question evokes comparison, analysis, differentiation. The concept *cuttlefish* emerges out of the matrix of the child's experience. The definition would be forgotten but the impression remains, and innumerable descriptive details are associated with it and remembered when the moment comes.

This is one element of the artistic pedagogical method. The child has learned instinctively that the whole expresses itself in every part, but that the whole is far more than the mere sum of its parts. He learns in his nine-year-old way to experience the reality of an idea. His intelligence has been spoken to by means of his imagination and feeling, an intelligence that, when fully awakened, will enable him to "see the wood" and not just so many trees. From the "whole to the part" is thus a main pedagogical nerve, but not only the presentation of a single lesson but the evolution of an entire subject curriculum follows this same dynamic.

Geometry is first experienced in motion. The first-grader runs the forms of a triangle, circle, square, pentagram in space. He knows with his entire body how different the turn of a right angle is from the sixty degrees of an equilateral triangle. Keeping equal distance from the center at every point on the circumference of a circle requires willpower, attention, and control, and it is the experience through the body that says "circle" to his six-year-old mind.

The experience of geometry is awakened at a new level in the sixth and seventh grades. Exact and beautiful constructions are developed and drawn with colored pencils. What was originally an encounter with geometric forms through the child's body and will is now transformed into an experience of the same geometric laws at work in the sphere of the aesthetic. Chiefly hands are active, acquiring discipline and skill. The constructions are practical, not yet abstract, but the laws speak through more clearly to the child's dawning comprehension. There is great joy in the discovery and perfection of each new form.

As the young person awakens to his own intelligence, geometry is reborn in the encounter with the self-sustaining truth of geometric laws experienced as pure thought-forms. The concepts that are the final fruit of a long process of learning are not abstract and dry. What was experienced through the body as a perceptual whole and reexperienced with artistic appreciation in the upper elementary grades resounds in the logical experience of the high school years.

The uninterrupted, two-hour *main lesson* with which each day begins is the academic cornerstone upon which the day is built. It encourages the child to become absorbed in, even saturated with, his subject—presented in the *block system*, for concentrated periods of four to six weeks. Recitational foreign-language lessons, practice lessons in English and arithmetic, music and eurythmy provide the more rhythmic element in the middle lessons of the day, and, as far as possible, the subjects engaging the child's bodily activity—physical education, sculpture, woodwork, practical laboratory, instrumental music—are scheduled in the afternoon. The exercise of the head, then the heart, and finally the active hands creates a healthy sequence that tires less and gives each day a rhythmic shape. Over many years, this helps the child to live with time, rather than against it.

This daily rhythm, which the child comes to know inwardly, is enforced by the rhythmic progression of new subjects and by the presence of a class teacher, who, whenever possible, continues with his or her class throughout the elementary grades. In an age of anonymity and scatteredness, the continuing class teacher shares with the parents the responsibility to protect and encourage, to discipline and to lead. A year is just the time it takes a teacher to really get to know a class, and the children to come to know and trust their teacher. These are among the most precious assets of a good year's work. Change teachers, and you start again from scratch. Just as the artistic method inevitably fosters good teachers, so the continuing role encourages increasing awareness of individual students and a broad span of skills.

Many schools today are in a hurry to train children young, and boast of the feats their five- or six-year-olds can perform. There seems little sense to this race. Often it dwarfs significant aspects of the child; too often it "finishes" him, prohibiting growth. The intellectual prodigy John Stuart Mill experienced a spiritual and emotional bankruptcy before twenty, and was deeply grateful to the poetry of Wordsworth for reviving the springs of feeling and reverence that should have been a more natural resource. Steiner would have a child simmer in his own juices awhile and develop strengths for a lifetime rather than exploit and deplete them foolishly.

Unlike the progressive schools, a Steiner school recognizes the basic need in children up to the age of fourteen for genuine authority—authority rooted in love and respect of child for teacher, and respect of the child's inherent self by the teacher, not authoritarianism.

The small child exerts unconscious energies never again equaled. He is a being of will and imitation, identifying himself with each gesture, intonation, mood, and thought of his environment, and making these his own in the free activity of creative imitative play. He is engaged in the great task of shaping and transforming his inheritance to individual and specific use. To divert these formative energies from their task in these early years is to weaken the vitality, undermine the health, and take from the developing child the endurance and strength he will need in adult life. Premature demands upon the intellect, sharp criticism, undue excitement of fantasy—as by television—and overstimulation of the senses combine to rob the child of his native physical resources. Given such a view of the preschooler, the kindergarten teacher's task becomes one of creating an environment worthy of a small child's unquestioning imitation. She educates the child's unconscious being through the warmth, the clarity, the rhythm, the harmony of the world she creates and with which he so actively identifies. Life speaks to the preschooler as gesture: he answers in creative play.

The little child longs to enjoy spontaneous freedom—but within the clearly defined security of order and form. He loves ceremony and regularity, and the comfort of careful attention to detail. He is, throughout the education, encouraged to really *see* objects and problems in their entirety, from all sides, in all their *thingness*. Under the right guidance, the preschooler brings a single-minded, almost religious devotion to the simplest activities of his daily existence. Tying his shoelace, lighting the candle before grace, the little mealtime verse and morning verse, scrubbing the doll corner, welcoming a guest— each act of the child is guided toward the beautiful, the ordered, the sacramental in life: and the children respond with enthusiasm and joy, full of "beans" and full of forms that encourage growth.

The end of the first phase of childhood, with its preoccupation with physical development, is signaled by the casting out of the baby teeth and their replacement with the far more individual second teeth, shaped out of the hardest substance of the bodily organism. Some parents balk at the emphasis on the teeth as a pivotal symbol—though most accept that an important change takes place at this time. At a Steiner school, the loss of teeth becomes, in a rather profound way, a status symbol!

With the first developmental phase complete, forces that have been engaged in the body are freed for a new kind of learning. Having shaped man's physical image, they are now liberated for use as the formative powers of imagination. Intelligence, which formerly educated the little child unconsciously, through his will and through his capacity for imitation, now feeds and shapes the elementary school child through his feelings. Everything that speaks to his imagination in pictures and stories, in color, rhythm, and music, is learned and remembered in such a way that it becomes a living part of him, is digested and becomes a *capacity for life*. The formative forces that remain active in the growing child now proceed from the head to take hold of the chest, harmonizing and individualizing the circulatory and breathing rhythms that provide the basis for the development of a normal and individual life of the emotions. These are the years in which every child, no matter what his gifts, is an artist at heart, and the teacher's task now becomes one of transforming intellectual knowledge into artistic experience. To the teacher who loves his art, the child brings unlimited devotion, accepting him gratefully as his authority, and accompanying him happily from year to year.

Letters are learned in the first grade as they originated: man perceived, then pictured, and out of the pictures abstracted signs and written symbols. The *m* of *mouth* and the *f* of *fish* are first transcribed as pictures of the top of a mouth and a fish, and letters emerge naturally from the images. The *Q* is encountered as the *Queen*, who, by the way, never forgets her *umbrella*, the *U*, which is always beside her. As the phonetic values of letters are drilled and drilled, the child repeats the original process with a sense of wonder, joy, discovery, and pride. The recitation and acting out of "I am a jolly Brother O," and so many other "games," engage the enthusiasm of play in the stern task of learning.

In the second grade, fables and legends are told and retold, acted out, and told individually in a child's own words—all greatly enhancing memory as well as imagination; in the third, stories from the Old Testament lead the children toward the study of history; then the Norse myths; the history of ancient civilizations culminating in Greece; Rome and medieval history; the Renaissance, the Reformation, and the Age of Discovery; and in the eighth grade, as the child reaches puberty, he catapults dramatically from the seventeenth century into the present—becomes nearer to being his own man in his own time.

Rudolf Steiner has said: "What is necessary is that through the medium of what is flexible and artistic we give the child in picture form, perceptions, ideas, and feelings which are capable of metamorphosis, which can grow together with the soul simply because the soul is growing." The pictures, the images of the stories that accompany and inform the study of and growth with history—so palpable and vivid—evoke a response far greater than that of merely the intellect at this stage; they become one with the child and stimulate growth.

What a child has learned, he instinctively wishes to reproduce and to form. Each child keeps a notebook record of his main-lesson studies and works at it at home, amplifying, condensing, restating, transcribing: actions that encourage and enforce the learning process. There is room for pictures, colorful margins, illuminated letters. Good penmanship is worth struggling for because one wants the book to be beautiful—a creation as well as a record. The artist in the child is touched, and his creative energies become a tremendous impetus to all further study.

This individual notebook significantly supplants the textbook in importance and further establishes the primarily inductive basis of Steiner education. Too often, textbooks offer merely the bald, hard facts of a subject—and eventually lie, like stones, in the stomach of learning; too often they become a substitute for thoughtful and urgent teaching, and for the child's own doing; and alas, too often they talk down to a common level of students and become plain dull.

The advent of puberty, with its marked emotional and physiological changes, signals the close of the second period of development. Again, a significant part of those forces that have been otherwise engaged are freed for learning, and the child's consciousness, which was at first active in the sphere of the will, and awoke in the life of feeling, now ascends at last into the pure realm of thought. The formative forces take hold of the limbs and lower organism. Hands and feet are enormous, arms and legs shoot down, lower jaws crop out, and inwardly, the young person is confronted with powers of feeling and will with which his newly emancipated capacity for intellectual intelligence must learn to cope. Out of the turmoil, his ego comes to a new experience of personal freedom—and education at this period must tap and channel, not stop up, the new energies. Authority is challenged, and the teacher must be ready to meet his student's need for competence, for authority vested in skill.

The need for independence in the high school is as natural as was the need for authority in the elementary years. Now the class teacher is replaced by subject teachers whose authority rests on their knowledge and experience. Here the appeal is directed increasingly to reasoned insight, intellectual understanding, a philosophic conception of the whole world. What was experienced pictorially, in a more artistic way, in the elementary years, now has to be reviewed, analyzed and tested in the light of the newly emerging power of personal, logical understanding.

But there is a marked continuity between the elementary and high school; like the adolescent to his earlier self, they are bound fast to each other, the one growing into the other. As the study of history is repeated, for instance, the adolescent is amazed and delighted with what he knows, and has felt, at earlier moments. Thus the history curriculum in the ninth grade deals with modern times, building on the foundations of four years of history study in the elementary grades. Then, in the tenth and eleventh grades, ancient and medieval civilizations are studied again, now at a more mature level, and the curriculum concludes with a review of world history in the senior year.

The high school curriculum is designed to lead into worldwide perspectives and into direct contact with the practical life of our day. The history of art, architecture, biology, advanced mathematics, chemistry, geography, literature, and history are among the subjects studied; and the students can now rise to the sweeping masterpieces of Sophocles, Aeschylus, Shakespeare, Goethe, and Melville—they go directly to the best and the broadest visions—as well as to the incisive study of the sciences. The objective capacity of thinking in both spheres—the sciences and the humanities—is trained.

Objective judgment is schooled through the year-by-year unfolding of the science curriculum. Its object is the education of a human being capable of becoming a scientist, not a scientist, a narrow specialist, who may no longer know how to become a human being. Furthermore, the teaching of science works from observation and comprehension of natural processes into a detailed understanding of the basic technology of our everyday life. Though the natural was stressed in the lower grades, it now becomes necessary to understand what man has wrought.

Thus the curriculum, especially in the upper grades, is strongly cumulative—the goal being a thoroughly grounded, whole human being. College preparation under this system is not an unrelated cramming but a review and confirmation of many years of work. Steiner graduates do well in the colleges and have gone to the best; but the Steiner goals are more fundamental, more permanent, than preparation for a specific group of colleges or for the taking of machinelike tests that now hold the moment: a Steiner education is for life.

This, in brief, is the logic of the artistic method in Rudolf Steiner education. It penetrates into the teaching of every subject in the school and challenges, by implication, all that is bleak and pictureless, artless and machinelike in the education of the young. Since life requires capacities, not theoretical concepts and abstract definitions, nor encyclopedic accumulations of information, its goal is the living concept. The artistic process leads to practice, repetition out of enthusiasm, and then to capacity and skill. Ultimately, it seeks to guide the natural devotion of the child to the world around him into an enthusiasm and love for beauty and knowledge, and, in later years, into reverence, love, and courage for the truth. It seeks true freedom—not the license that parades under that name, but an inner self-fulness bred of discipline and gradually unfolded talents. "Our highest endeavor," Rudolf Steiner said, "must be to develop free human beings, who are able of themselves to impart purpose and direction to their lives."

Actually, freedom and individual responsibility operate in the very structure of the school, for its faculty exist truly as a community of equals, taking full responsibility for the operation of their school, electing their own chairman (in place of the traditional appointed principal or headmaster) and pursuing their own excellence. Some teachers devise their own playlets and stories for the class; all operate creatively within the broad Steiner outline. In a world in which slavery by the state, slavery by machine, slavery by ignorance, slavery to passions and drugs, and slavery by boredom are so rampant, the Steiner School's pursuit of spiritual freedom is the more significant—and rare.

The Steiner or Waldorf method is neither flawless nor static. It has practical as well as theoretical challenges. Qualified, devoted, trained teachers are hard to find; many of its schools have modest, even inadequate physical plants; and the ideas themselves, in their practical application, constantly undergo development and modification—for the last thing Rudolf Steiner himself wanted was a "system" to which interested persons rendered themselves slavishly bound.

Most students who go on to college marvel at how much of their learning is actually a part of them, how much it is a resource upon which to draw, a guide to full and responsive living. Again—a school fulfills its function to the extent that its teaching is transformed into creative capacities for life.

Gratitude to the divine world out of which the small child enters life; love for the art of teaching in the elementary years; respect for a young person's spiritual freedom—these three attitudes, understood and practiced by the teachers, can lead to a true education in each of the three stages of a child's development. And for the child who has been so understood and aided in his unfolding, it is to be hoped that the man he fathers will now be able to "impart purpose and direction" to his own life, that he will have his childhood powers intact, his sense of wonder touched, his respect for and pursuit of excellence a permanent resource, and his moral fiber firm and free.

• • •

In the essays that follow—all written by teachers or former teachers at American Steiner schools—you will catch glimpses of Waldorf education at work. The book does not attempt to capture all aspects of the pedagogy but to share and let readers "see" some of them.

Joy and happiness in living, a love of all existence, a power and energy for work—such are among the lifelong results of a right cultivation of the feeling for beauty and for art.

— RUDOLF STEINER

THE SEEDS OF SCIENCE

Margaret de Ris

Before planning on how we may bring an experience of science to preschool children, we must have a clear picture of the way in which this age group behaves. When we observe four-year-olds at play, the most outstanding characteristic is first their constant activity, and it is in this "always doing" that the small child orientates himself to the physical world and experiments with the physical world. To satisfy this urge we must supply the children with material that they can handle, explore, and shape to their needs. Second, there is their tremendous enthusiasm and interest in everything about them. There isn't anything too trivial to merit their attention or too far above to escape the eternal question "why?" The four-year-old has the true spirit of the scientist and philosopher. He is open-minded, without prejudice, and questions the "why" of everything. Third, the preschool child approaches life in a subjective way. He identifies himself with the world about him and in his play shapes and makes things over to suit his imagination. It is the period of "make-believe," and we must be extremely careful not to burden the small child with a lot of factual knowledge, and instead supply experiences that make him wonder and think about the world and give him a chance to work out his own curiosity. The most delicate role of the teacher is to watch for these seeds of curiosity and then nurture them with appropriate experiences that will satisfy this curiosity.

The desired objectives in bringing an experience of science to children are, first, to help the child adjust himself to the world in which he is to live; second, to eliminate superstitions and unscientific ideas as well as unreasonable fears; third, to foster in him an attitude of questioning and experimentation; and fourth, to lead him ever more deeply into a feeling of kinship with nature.

Our school is fortunate in its location just half a block from Central Park, and our daily excursions to the park provide excellent opportunity for experimentation and investigation. The children become keenly aware how their beloved late-summer flowers gradually disappear and the leaves fall to the ground. As winter passes and ice and snow gradually disappear, the children wait with eager interest for the approaching signs of spring. They observe that the ground changes. It is no longer hard and frozen but becomes soft and moist. Gradually, here and there the grass shows signs of green, and small buds appear on trees. In the fall the children are given full freedom to play with the leaves, rake them in piles, collect them, and discover differences. We take with us our baskets and look for nuts under some of the trees, acorns under others, and long beans under still others. Back in school we empty our treasures onto special shelves and the children hunt eagerly though the pages of our big tree book for pictures of these same fruits. Before long they know the names of several of the trees and it becomes a game to see how many of the trees they can identify. We also observe the squirrels busily collecting acorns and learn that they are preparing for the winter. We notice that most of our songbirds have disappeared and learn that they have gone further south where there is no hard winter and where they will find the food they need. This leads to an interesting discussion as to the type of birds, what foods they eat, and how they travel. There are quite a number of charming stories that make this whole subject very much alive. The children also miss some of our little friends, like the chipmunk, and learn that they have gone to sleep for the winter.

The children show tremendous interest in every phase of nature. What we adults have come to take for granted to the small child still holds the greatest wonder and delight—the wind pushing and carrying him, to watch the clouds chasing through the sky, to listen to the sound of the rain, the deep silence of the falling snow—all these experiences are full of newness and fascination for him. It is up to us as teachers to foster and nurture this closeness the child has with nature.

Central Park, with its multitude of experiences, is our outdoor laboratory. Here we can combine vigorous play with quiet individual observation. While climbing the big rocks we also become aware of the special crystals contained in some of the rocks and the mica glistening in the sun. We come to handle some of the rocks and observe that some stones are very hard while others crumble to dust. Whenever we discover something particularly interesting we take it back to our science corner, where we can all study it together. In digging in the ground we observe that there are places where there is pure sand that has been washed down the hill after the pouring rain, while in other sections the earth is black and heavy. We spent some time in a secluded section of the park making miniature gardens. The children collected flowers and small branches and, using these for trees, created charming little enclosures framed by stones they had laboriously collected. The most important educational feature resulting from this play came the next day when the children returned and found the rain had completely washed away the earth, leaving deep gullies where their gardens had been. The children were amazed by the force of the rain. Another rather illuminating outdoor experience was a trip to a nearby small truck garden. We took a few children at a time and they had their first glimpse, among other things, into the building up of a compost pile. They observed how nothing was wasted but everything added to this pile, from kitchen garbage to leaf mold. The children were allowed to help load the wheelbarrow and empty it onto the compost pile. They were much impressed to see what had happened to the garbage of the preceding year and how it had been miraculously transformed into black earth.

Within our classroom we have tried to give the children as many different experiences of nature as possible. Our old sandbox has been turned into an indoor garden where we experiment with all sorts of seeds. The most satisfactory has been just ordinary canary seed, which shows almost immediate results. We also have a section where we try carrot greens, sweet potatoes, and similar plants. The children thoroughly enjoy watching for signs of the seeds, and the area is big enough that they can use the watering can to their heart's content. We also try experiments with bulbs, placing them first into a dark closet and then, when they have started to sprout, bringing them into the light. The children take real interest in observing the shoots change to green when they are brought into the light. They also observe how the blossoms turn toward the sun.

We have a large-sized terrarium with different colorful plants. The children soon ask why the plants in the terrarium do not need watering and are interested when they raise the cover to see drops of moisture. This gives them a slight intimation of the meaning of rain. In the terrarium we have a few red newts, a tiny snake, and two turtles. These little creatures are a great attraction; the children particularly enjoy watching the turtle and are fascinated by the way in which the legs, head, and tail completely disappear in the shell. We also have an aquarium with two goldfish—very colorful ones with large tails, a few snails, and tadpoles. The tadpoles are especially interesting and the children watch with eager interest for the little feet to appear and the gradual transition to the frog stage.

We were very fortunate last spring in discovering a large cocoon in the park, which we kept in our classroom. One morning when almost all the children were present, one youngster noticed a slight movement in the cocoon, and after about an hour's struggle there emerged the most beautiful moth, much to the delight and almost startling surprise of the children. They were trembling with excitement and it was an experience that most of them will remember for many years to come.

We have tried to give the children experiences with a variety of small animals suitable to the classroom. The most successful were a pair of white rats that were very friendly and could be relied on not to bite. It was a good experience for some of the children to actually hold a small animal. The timid child would more easily forget his own fear and in identifying himself with the animal would feel bigger and stronger himself. It is also a very important experience for small children to learn how to hold and handle an animal without hurting it. The children learned to realize that these lit-tle creatures just didn't like noise and confusion and would stay in their house until the excitement died down. We have had the visit of a kitten that one of the children brought in, a pair of hamsters lent by Hunter College laboratory, a variety of turtles and frogs, and a pair of guinea pigs. We didn't keep any of these animals, with the exception of the rats, more than a week, partly to retain the children's lively interest, but also to make the children aware that it isn't kind to keep these little visitors too long in captivity. The children learned to feed them, to clean them, and also took part in the responsibility of keeping cages properly closed to save them from the cat.

An important factor in the children's relationship to plant and animal life in the class-room is the element of repetition. We try to have our experiences with nature as much as possible at the same hour every day and cover much the same ground. Each child or group of children has a special task—to water plants, loosen earth around plants, give water and food to animal visitors, collect leftover foods for them, help clean cages, and similar tasks. In talking about animals we try to develop an understanding of the rela-tionship of different animals to wildlife—as dog to wolf, cat to lion—of what we mean by the word *animal* as differentiated from *plant* and *stone*, and of the different types of animals, birds, and fish.

Water, with all its tremendous possibilities, is one of the best materials for experi-mentation. A rubber tube with which the child can siphon water from a higher container to a lower one gives endless opportunity for scientific discovery—so does any variety of water play. The main thing is to allow the child as much freedom as possible without the feeling of hurry or the worry about clothes, for instance.

A sieve allows for any number of experiments with water as well as sand. Watercolors also lead to a variety of interesting experiences with color that the child can bring about at will.

In regard to all approaches to science with preschool children, we try to avoid ever burdening them with facts and information. Information is only given when the child asks for it and then to the extent that it really holds his interest. The small child's rela-tion to science is an entirely different one from that of the older child or adult. The four-and five-year-olds are still close to the baby stage, where experiences are closely connect-ed with bodily sensations, such as tasting, touching, and handling. Our analytical approach does not satisfy them, nor are they satisfied by merely watching, but they must take an active part. I found that it is most valuable for this age to have the satisfaction of personal discovery and the possibility of applying this discovery to their dramatic play.

In our music period we have made use of any number of ways of producing sound from improvised drums to wires strung across two nails.

The possibilities for scientific experiences in preschool are practically limitless, and the important point to me has been to supply the children with an atmosphere that is conducive to quiet experimentation. Our duty is to help the child clarify his ideas and in this way avoid many later fears and superstitions. The small child has had little experience and will identify himself with everything he hears and sees. For example, during one of our experiences with seeds, a little boy was much troubled when he saw some beans sprout. Inquiring into it, we found the child had formed the erroneous conclusion that some beans he had consumed the night previous for dinner would sprout in his stomach. This led to a rather interesting experiment where we cooked different seeds and then planted them.

We have also experimented with ice and the effect of ice on glass jars. The children were much surprised to see that ice floats in water and that liquids expand when freezing. We had a graphic illustration of this when our milk was left outside the building one extremely cold morning and we found tall whitecaps on the tops of the bottles. This led to a series of experiments with freezing. Then there is of course the endless fun of breaking ice puddles, and of lying on the ice on the pond when it is thick and like glass and peering down into the clear water below and seeing life. This makes a deep impression on every child.

There is little the small child busies himself with that doesn't in some way enter the field of science—from the use of cylindrical blocks for moving heavy boxes to experimenting with equilibrium on the seesaw or with friction by rubbing two stones together. The most important thing is not so much which experience we emphasize, but that we develop human beings who will not be afraid to try things, who will be explorative and have confidence in themselves.

THE TRUE MEANING OF DISCIPLINE

Nanette Grimm

When we speak of a class we are, in my opinion, necessarily speaking of discipline; for in its simplest form a class is a group of children who, in our case, come together to learn. Of course, learning may take place in many situations, but it is the specific purpose of a class. It is in "learning" that what I believe to be the true meaning of discipline lies. With the class and for the class, the teacher strives to create as ideal a learning situation as he can, out of his knowledge of and his relationship to the children.

With the very young children who live in the world of imitation, the teacher creates a fairy-tale atmosphere and lives in it with her children. She works with them and plays with them, for through her attitude in all she says and does the children learn. When she wishes them to do some modeling work, she puts out the clay and boards around the table and she herself sits down and takes a piece of clay and begins to fashion a rabbit or turtle or whatever, and very soon the children flock around her, eagerly wanting to use the clay, too. When it is time to go upstairs to rest period, the children must go quietly, they must be relaxed. If in her attitude, the teacher says something like, "Now, children, you will walk upstairs without a word and lie down on your beds quietly," they will probably do just that, but where is the relaxation? How can they really rest under this tension? If, on the other hand, she says, "We are all little mice who creep upstairs and into our beds so that no one in the house hears us" (it matters not so much what she says as how she says it), if she is quiet and walks on tiptoes, all the little mice will follow along, and will love it and will want to do it every time; it will be "the" way to go upstairs and they will be prepared to rest. The teacher, appealing to the children out of their particular stage of development, acting within the realm of her relationship to them, has created the mood. So the learning takes place, the discipline is right, and what we may call discipline problems are reduced to a minimum—they are individual.

As the children grow older, as they increase in ability and independence, as they gradually advance to a new stage of development, their way of learning gradually changes, and a different approach and a new kind of relationship between class and teacher are required. How shall the best mood for learning now be created? If instruction or direction is given, if a question is asked or an answer is given, the class must be able to listen—to listen with complete attention, not playing with something in the desk or poking at a neighbor, but in a fully concentrated way. Aside from removing as many external distractions as possible, including the playthings in the desk or even the bothersome neighbor (which is really a protection for the child), the teacher must herself be fully concentrated. All her efforts must go in the direction of her class. Real concentration is refreshing; it does not tire as halfhearted efforts do, and so the teacher strives to call forth the wholehearted enthusiasm of the children, to capture and hold their attention by appealing through the lively, living realm of the imagination. The imaginative approach is what the children are longing for at this age, and whatever is presented in such a way is satisfying to them, they respond to it with enthusiasm, they say "YES" to it, and learning is joy!

It must be remembered, however, that the children's span of concentration in any one kind of activity is limited. If a class is kept at mental arithmetic for too long a period, no matter how interested or attentive they have been, they will grow restless and inattentive and begin to squirm or chatter or play with their fingers or their ears; Johnny will ask permission to get a drink, followed by half a dozen others, or Betty will ask, "Will you please tell us a story?" They need a change! To continue with this activity is not only fruitless, it can be damaging. The children will not learn, for the mood originally created no longer exists, and a persistent "to the bitter end" attitude of the teacher either irritates the children further or sends them into a dull stupor; as the teacher pushes harder, the children become tense; there is no learning, the discipline is wrong, and out of such situations discipline problems that would not ordinarily exist arise.

So the plan, the structure, the form of the day is a most important factor in learning, in discipline. The children need a balance of activity. A change renews them after concentrated effort and they are eager to go on to the next phase of the work. There must be a sort of breathing, a flow from one kind of activity to another: the thinking and the doing, the quiet and the lively. As I overheard one of my children telling another, "There is a time to be noisy and a time to be quiet," and so there is! Children need "breaks," perhaps even more so than do grown-ups. You know how many coffee breaks adults take in the course of a day, and we call it "catching a breath."

Even the best approach and the most carefully arranged form of the day's activities will be effective only if there exists the proper relationship between the children and the teacher. Her mistakes and failings (and after all, fortunately, teachers are human and do make mistakes) are forgiven and taken in good spirit if her basic connection to the children is right. This relationship, I think, depends fundamentally upon a genuine love and respect for the child as well as a strong guidance; the firm but loving hand, the loving but firm hand—both qualities are essential. Without the firmness, the children do not receive the control they need when they are incapable of self-control. They need boundaries set for them by someone whom they feel has a deep concern for them. Within these boundaries they find protection and security; they can relax and give themselves over freely to the adventures of learning. They want to know what they may or may not do, whether in class work, lining up, or playing in the park. They want to test the limits and they respect and appreciate someone who consistently but lovingly holds them to these limits. Without the love, the firmness can become a pressure, a bearing down upon the children. They become tense and cross, unable therefore to concentrate, so while they may "behave," they do not learn and grow to their full abilities. The teacher who holds a class in this fashion becomes a rather ridiculous figure to the children, and while they may appear to be listening with placid expressions, they are probably planning some gruesome prank to play upon her.

Perhaps the most valuable asset in dealing with children is a sense of humor!

Now, I haven't at all mentioned correction or punishment, which are, after all, a part of learning, of discipline. Children have strengths and weaknesses and the teacher deals with the weaknesses as well as the strengths. But I think correction is primarily an individual matter that is worked out through the understanding of the child and his particular problems, and the situation at hand. In speaking of what would be called a normal, healthy class with a reasonable normal, healthy teacher, where there is knowledge and understanding of children and their development out of which emerges the proper approach and the right form of the class activities, where there is a right relationship between the children and teacher, there the most favorable mood for learning is created, there the discipline is right.

THE WINDOWS OF THE LOWER SCHOOL

Virginia E. Paulsen

The building at 15 East Seventy-ninth Street appears to the average New Yorker as an ordinary, gray sandstone structure, having its counterpart throughout the neighborhood. The teachers who work within and the children who have attended the Rudolf Steiner School for a number of years know that this is not so, for our school is unique. It glows and sparkles from within and without with many worlds.

Look at the school with the imaginative eye of the teacher. First, there is a garden in which the littlest children play. Castles are in this garden for the small princesses and princes. There are forests with dragons that must be slain and giants to be outwitted. There are houses in which children can sweep and clean, where dollies are loved and cared for. Here a child can imitate all the wonderful actions of the adults in the world around him. Everywhere there is an intensity of color: the warm gold of the sun, the pure blue of the sky, the strong red of courage. The children live and breathe in the colors and the colors speak to them.

Look further. Above the garden rises a golden octagonal house, and this is the Rudolf Steiner School for children between the ages of six and fourteen. It is a building of many windows, but these are not the windows one expects to see on Seventy-ninth Street, windows adorned with curtains and pots of geranium, nor are they the kind that let in the city breezes and noises. They are very special windows. Every day in the eight rooms, the teachers build them anew and open them for the children. Each child sees a slightly different view, depending upon his individual temperament, but each view is carefully directed by the teacher. The windows are never rose-colored; they are always crystal clear.

What do the children see? Enter the golden octagonal house and look with them into the windows. In the first room a fish is seen swimming gaily about. Suddenly it changes from a fish into the picture of the beginning of fish, or *F*. Perhaps a raindrop has fallen from a cloud upon a mountaintop and the children watch its adventuresome journey as it finds its way into a brook, a stream, a river, and at last into the vast ocean from which the friendly sun lifts it once more up into the heavens.

Before the eyes of the second-graders the world of the fable unfolds. Foolish crows are flattered by sly foxes; flighty hares are beaten by purposeful tortoises. In the third grade the great figures of the Old Testament in all their majesty are witnessed. On this day the waters of the Red Sea have parted and Moses is leading the Children of Israel to safety. There are other sights for the third-graders, too. Farmers sow their grains, milk the cows, feed their chickens; Indians build wickiups and masons construct a little brick house.

When a child enters the fourth room, he sees the golden city of Asgard as well as forbidding Jotunheim, the land of the giants. Many members of the animal kingdom appear and the child can look with awe right into all four stomachs of the cow. One day when the teacher opens the window, the fourth grade sees Manhattan, perhaps even Seventy-ninth Street, as it appeared three hundred years ago, and watches it develop up to the present day.

In the fifth grade the children's eyes are filled with tears, for Socrates is bidding his friends farewell and is preparing to drink the hemlock poison. Next month they will be able to relax as they watch a tulip grow and gaze with wonder at the star in its blossom. The children in the sixth room are stirred by the military tactics of the Roman legions. Soon they will be horrified at the cruelty of the Roman games and the persecution of the Christians and Jews. At another time they will see the tremendous mouth of the Amazon and trace it through the dense Brazilian jungles to its source in the high Andes. The seventh grade watches in fascination as Martin Luther hurls an ink pot at the devil. Their blood is chilled by the evil cleverness of the Medici, but in another lesson they will be thrilled by the sight of Norway's glaciers and fjords. The eighth grade gazes into all four corners of the world and they see what is happening right at the moment. Perhaps their teacher has guided their vision to the miseries of the homeless in Hong Kong, where whole families sleep in the streets. They have watched Abraham Lincoln pace up and down, his shoulders bowed with the tragic burden of a whole nation.

These are fragmentary glimpses of what might be seen in the wonderful windows found in the golden octagonal house that is the Rudolf Steiner School. It is not the handsome gray stone building; it is not the fine white marble staircase nor the new stage with its red curtains; it is not the wooden desks and chairs, the library, or the efficient lunchroom; it is not the special equipment, the latest textbooks, the many degrees of its faculty. None of these is of special value. It is, however, the opened, light-filled windows that make our school unique—the windows of the mind, of the heart, and of the spirit. When the children have passed through all the eight grades and prepare to enter high school, they take, as a special gift, these opened windows with them.

THE CLASS TEACHER

Tim Hoffmann

A few years ago, in the last weeks of the school year, I met with the parents of the children who were to become the new first grade. The idea that one teacher would stay with the class was not new to them. But in actually meeting the person who would fulfill that role, a certain sense of the scope of this new relationship seemed to dawn in the minds of these parents. So we spent the evening in discussion, getting to know each other. We examined the reasons why such a long relationship might be helpful. Parents asked—politely—what would happen if their child and I would not get along. They wanted to know how I would address the full spectrum of academic skills in the class, how I would deal with boys and girls, how I would try to make the curriculum relevant, how I would assess the children's progress, and such like. Such were the concerns of this particular parent group regarding the question of the class teacher. What follows is a summary of my comments to them, my attempts to clarify the school's aims and to foster enthusiasm for this grand undertaking.

To begin with, I asked the parents to imagine their children as fourteen-year-olds. At the time of the meeting they were six. What changes did they anticipate? The physical ones would be obvious. But what of the soul and spiritual aspects? And what of their relationship to authority? Could the parents imagine life with a budding adolescent at home?

The conversation flowed freely, and we all felt that the beginning of a long process had been witnessed. We came to imagine this process as part of the birth of the child's individuality. We, it was clear, were to be midwives during this second seven-year cycle, the time of the elementary school years.

Without doubt, the eight-year teaching cycle is one of the most well known facets of Waldorf education. Since the founding in 1919, when Rudolf Steiner suggested that the class teacher remain with the same group of children from first through eighth grade, Waldorf schools have distinguished themselves by placing so much responsibility on one person's shoulders.

Why do this? What are the advantages?

The elementary school years coincide roughly with the second seven-year cycle of life. From the time when a child is ready for grade school to the beginning of her secondary education, a particular style of learning reigns. Although it goes through several clearly defined variations, the common denominators of these stages are openness to the beauty in all things and a willingness to turn to an authority figure for guidance. As understood by Waldorf teachers, authority represents the best of the adult world into which the child desires to grow. Thus, the class teacher's authority is neither disciplinarian nor dogmatic. Rather, it represents to the youngster everything that is devoted to beauty in art, to truth in science, to caring for the welfare of the group and awareness of the individual's needs. He loves his work and never shows a cynical attitude. In his love of learning he embodies an enthusiasm (literally, in-spiriting) before the students' eyes. He is as attuned to the current affairs in the world around him as he is to the soul life of his students.

Keeping in mind the changes in attitude children undergo during the elementary school years, one might be led to question whether such a single figure can truly serve them from beginning to end. The Waldorf community is in fact discussing whether it is appropriate in light of the changing demands being made on schools, both by parents and by students. The arguments being made in favor of such a review can be summarized as follows:

- Parents generally side with their children in disputes with the school.

- Teachers' authority is often undermined by parents who question the school's policies more frequently and vocally than before.

- Few teachers feel prepared to handle so many parental concerns and criticisms.

- The academic demands on the teacher of the upper elementary grades are often beyond the teacher's means.

- Children manifest attitudes that can be considered precocious, and teachers' fairness and wisdom is challenged by increasingly younger pupils.

- On the home front, it appears that parents are less intuitive regarding their children.

- More parent education is needed from the teachers.

Thus, the challenge teachers face is taking on new characteristics. To what degree is the Waldorf system still adequate/appropriate? One could respond with these considerations in favor of the class teacher's role:

- Precisely because childhood seems less secure, a central figure can be a source of stability.

- Precocity is accompanied by a need to be understood and supported and is not akin to maturity.

- The close relationship between student and class teacher allows for more meaningful assessment of academic progress, for more individualized help with parents.

- In creating the main lesson plan, the class teacher integrates a wealth of material into a whole, and the problems of compartmentalization are avoided.

- Over the course of eight years, a metamorphosis of the content occurs. This coincides with the student's development and reinforces her sense that she is recognized both individually and as part of the human family.

The narrative developed and presented by the teacher underscores all of the above.

The complexities of the discussion bring us back to the fundamental question of education: what is its purpose?

If one goes beyond the obvious goals of developing skills, moral integrity, self-confidence, and the like, what is left? Don't we have as an ideal behind all our work as teachers that we are helping our students to become fully human in the broadest possible sense? That we are helping them on a path of individuation that must follow a certain rhythm of unfolding? That to work against that rhythm is to hurt the child? For example, when do we serve the child's interest by encouraging decision making? Or, when is the concept of causality within a child's intellectual reach? Or, when can one expect the child to interpret works of literature analytically? Or understand and comment on political events? The answers to all of these are the same: at the right age they can and must all be expected. But if they are asked too early, such demands can be harmful. The child is slowly being born into the workings of the adult mind. To demand abstraction from a mind that is not yet mature is to rob the soul of the security it experiences in its still-pictorial understanding of the world. The soul life of children in their seventh year, the time when they meet their class teacher, is still at one with their environment. At this age the child not only identifies strongly with the world she perceives, she enlivens everything with human qualities. They are profoundly sure of the inherent goodness of their world. One need only think of the fairy tales the class teacher tells at this age; these all end with a reattainment of a paradisal state in which everything is in order. There is no room for moral ambiguity; good triumphs over evil. In the first year of the class teacher's connection with the children, such stories help to form a bond. But even fairy tales lose their appropriateness as the children become wise to the subtleties of social and emotional questions. Thus, the curricular outline for the narrative in each grade is chosen in such a way that it might mirror the inner development of the individual. The great literature of the early epochs thus forms the bulk of the third, fourth, and fifth grades' story curriculum. In general, these epics portray a gradual emancipation of the human spirit from a divine but authoritarian leadership. From Bible stories to the beginnings of historicity in classical Greece, the conflicts the teacher chooses to present to the class form a stream of development that nurtures the individual in her struggle to find herself. What joy a youngster experiences upon hearing of Alexander the Great's success. But also the sorrow of Dido's self-immolation. The delight in hearing of Loki's pranks can be contrasted with the righteous sense of justice she feels when punishment is meted out. And so on.

Here the reader might interject, this is all well and good, but why must it be the same teacher from year to year, when surely a greater variety would be provided if they were to change. Although the point has merit, it misses the central issue. The choice and manner of presentation of stories must vary according to each class. If they are to have pedagogical merit, the story must come alive in the moment of telling. It is not read from the printed page, but is described in vivid pictures that the teller creates. These will be painted in a way the class needs. Even Alexander's greatness can be tempered by his vanity, as might the description of Dido's end be spared the graphic detail. And for those ten-year-olds whose enjoyment of Loki's punishment seems heartless, the teacher can develop a greater sense of empathy in choosing the next story.

Even once the students have reached the upper elementary school years, when story as such is less appropriate, the telling biographies come to play a similar role for the class. The teacher who knows his students and their school history will know what life story will best suit his class. It would be counterproductive to prescribe a set of biographies for certain ages; no two classes are alike.

What has been described here in relation to the narrative content also applies to the other aspects of his work with the children. For example, in the language arts, the skills developed in grade one are intimately connected to the grammar lessons in grade four. How the child learned to read will tell the teacher a great deal about how he can expect the child to learn the use of the tenses. Different learning styles, if recognized and understood by the teacher, are a key to teaching the children. For one child, repeated hearing and practice are required to learn a new skill. For another, visual memory is strong, and working in a beautiful main lesson book is the key. Other students simply require time and typically only understand new concepts the second or third time through. Here, too, it is most helpful if the teacher can be with his children long enough to develop this understanding. It is needed in all subjects.

Another example may be helpful. At the time of writing this essay, I am preparing a geography main lesson for my sixth grade. The subject is South America. I must determine what aspects to emphasize, whether cultural, economic, anthropological, and so on. But however I design these lessons, I know I must take into account the previous year's experiences. What went well and what didn't? What connections can be made to the other disciplines? History? Math? Research papers? Music? And so forth. In short, the lateral integration of the subjects, as well as the integration and development over time, form the basis of my preparations and teaching. But the continuity depends on my input. This is the class teacher's role.

A reader may suggest that anyone promoting such an idea is deluding himself and ignoring the pitfalls of personal weakness and bias, and this seems a fair objection. And, indeed, when class teachers have experienced difficulties, those have tended to arise from personal issues that have obtruded on the teaching. This is where a study of Steiner's work in spiritual science is important. Although there is no creed to which teachers subscribe, no set of beliefs that is a prerequisite to become a teacher, the aspect of self-development, at least in its preliminary form, must be considered. Steiner wrote and spoke at various times of the possibilities one has as an adult to gain greater control over one's soul life. The six attributes he places at the beginning demand of the practitioner that he gain discipline in his thinking, equanimity in his feeling life, and more conscious control over his will. To these Steiner adds that the student should work to develop the attitudes of positiveness and receptivity. Striving toward these goals is, on the one hand, the surest way for a teacher to prepare himself for the many challenges to be faced. More important, though, he will become more attuned to the subtleties that present themselves in the demeanor and behavior of his students. Our goal, as we help the children on their paths of individuation, begins with the acknowledgment and recognition of their genius. This is the work in anthroposophy.

Class teaching is an established part of our school's program. As with all programs, though, there is a risk of falling into routine. The original sense of purpose is easily lost. To remain effective, teachers must strive constantly to renew their enthusiasm and to deepen their understanding.

Now, with the celebration of our seventy-fifth year, it is all the more urgent that we reinvigorate our teaching. Waldorf education, and with it the concept, was first manifest in 1919. But the roots of our work lie in the twenty-first century. Our work will succeed if we keep in touch with contemporary culture and contemporary childhood.

FAIRY TALES IN THE FIRST GRADE

Dorothy Harrer

"Tell us a story!" is the demand of the children after their first days in school in which they have found, to their great joy, that fairy tales have a part in their lessons. Without a doubt the time they like best is the time when the teacher says, "Put your chairs in a nice round circle and get ready for a story."

At once all efforts converge to make this moment come quickly and, as soon as we are all sitting in the circle, the children settle down in a way that means, "We'd rather be here than anywhere else."

As for the teacher, this is the time when she can claim the most wholehearted attention, and so, within the imaginations of the story, deal with the inner life of the class as in no other way. To say "wholehearted attention" does not give adequate description of what happens in the children as they listen to a fairy tale. They go beyond attention into a much more active state. They hardly notice the storyteller for the story. As one tells a story one sees that no matter how lively one's feeling may be for what one tells, the children are far more active in their listening than the teacher is in the telling. For instance, in the midst of a story-battle between the prince and the seven-headed dragon, a small boy will suddenly leap out of his chair and strike the dragon's head off; or when Hansel says to Gretel, in the dark forest, "Don't cry, little sister, I will take care of you," one sees the sad tears rolling down the cheeks of a certain little girl; or again when in the story a little gnome falls down, down, down into a deep hole in the ground and lands "bump" at the bottom, another little girl turns into a gnome and suddenly falls off her chair to land on the floor in the middle of the circle, which has become for her the bottom of the hole.

And so it is that the wonderful range of feeling that weaves in every fairy tale becomes an activity within the children. If, at first, this happens only when you are telling the stories, it gradually comes about that it begins to happen at other times as an echo of the stories, and finally it appears in the children's own imaginations to enliven them.

At the beginning of the year the children were somewhat at a loss as to what to play at recess. They played stoop-tag, they played train, some of them knew only how to play at shooting guns. All of them had little inclination to stay together in a game. It was hard for them to make up their minds what to play and then to play it all the way through. The teacher showed them how to play Nuts in May, Red Rover, Swinging Statues. She helped them act out some of the fairy tales, but it meant that she had to hover over every character to tell each one what he should say or do. Then, after Christmas, there was a surprising change.

It happened most unexpectedly one rainy day when recess was indoors. The teacher looked up from some work at the desk to see the whole class standing in royal splendor on the small stage at one end of the room. Each child had draped a piece of colored cloth around him. Each child wore a paper crown, or paper wings, or carried a paper sword. There they were deep in affairs of state: kings and queens, princes and princesses, lords and ladies, all in order. Then with *the* queen leading the way, they walked in stately fashion from "palace" to "garden" to "palace" again, conversing in a lofty mood.

And so it began. After that there was never any question of what to do at recess. Day after day, for the rest of the year, they made up their play themselves and roamed the park as kings and queens, giants and witches, messengers and gnomes. In all their eager activity one saw that through the fairy tales their imaginations had been touched and awakened in much the same way that the Prince once awakened the Sleeping Beauty.

Why do the fairy tales do this more than any other sort of story?

When a fairy tale has been told by the teacher, the children are asked to retell it the next day. A comparison was made between their memory of Grimm's fairy tales and those well-thought-out "here and now" stories that describe *real life* in a way suited to children. No matter how long the fairy tale is, the children can remember its colorful pictures and its rhythmically recurring events, and they can retell it almost word for word. When they have been asked to retell a story that rises from a logical thought pattern, they answer again and again, "Oh, that's a hard story, we can't remember it."

Take, for instance, a typical story of a little boy who goes to visit his grandfather on a farm. He sees the dog, the cat, the pig, the calf, and all the other farm animals, and they are described realistically. Then follows some sort of adventure during the course of which the little boy is kind to animals. Compare all such realistic, moralistic stories with any one of Grimm's fairy tales and what do you find? In the fairy tales, all the human qualities of courage, honesty, warmth of heart, and kindness are opposed by trickery, treachery, cruelty, and folly. These qualities appear as kings and soldiers, witches and dwarves, giants and dragons. Event after event unfolds in which these beings play their part to carry the children with them through all the adventures of the realm of human moral feeling.

The storyteller, parent or teacher, can develop a sense for the difference between stories that create an inner activity and those that don't. In stories that have a rhythmic repetition of events that follow one another in a pictorial and often *un*-logical way, the children are enlivened. Stories that have the effect of going on and on—in which situations develop for logical purposes, in which thoughts are called upon to make sense—clearly baffle the children. The rhythmic and pictorial qualities of the fairy tale rise directly from the realm of feeling. This reality of the fairy tale claims the children at an age when feeling is their guide. In comparison, the "here and now" stories that describe the "real" world in a scientific way have the effect of keeping the children out of the story, for it is not true that the scientific view (no matter if it is in three-letter words) must be impersonal. And when you are tempted to tell a moralizing story, just remember that it will make children with healthy feeling want to run away.

The fairy tales avoid this, and in the way in which they exercise and educate children in the human moral realm they bring to the first year of schoolwork something that must be recognized more and more as a necessary element of education. In an age when brilliance of mind has failed to create any understanding of the connection between moral feeling and knowledge, it is of great importance for the future that education should make this connection by planting in the fields of a knowledge-of-the-world the seed that is the knowledge of the human being as a moral being.

The fairy tales do this. At the heart of each fairy tale lies a kernel of wisdom about man. And this wisdom nourishes the children. They are truly hungry for it.

One can point to this as the inner content of the work of the first grade in the Rudolf Steiner School, and at the same time show how the fairy tales lend themselves to the teachings of the three Rs, as well as to painting, modeling, and dramatics.

The forms of the letters of the alphabet are taught in such a way as to show how they emerge out of picture shapes. The *W* is a *wave* in the sea where swims the prince, enchanted as a fish. The *butterflies*, asleep in the palace gardens while Briar Rose sleeps, give the shape of the letter *B*. The seven *mountains*, which are traveled by the witch and the seven dwarfs in the story of Snow White, become *M*s. One sees how these imaginations of things are better teachers than the things themselves would be. Small children pay scant heed to the shapes of actual objects in comparison with the rapt attention they give to the story of the wicked witch who comes over the seven mountains to bring Snow White a poisoned apple.

In arithmetic, stories like "The Seven Ravens" and "The Twelve Dancing Princesses" can be used to dramatize various number relationships.

In painting and in modeling with colored plasticine, the fairy tales give an unlimited variety of subjects for developing artistic skills.

The teacher learns from the fairy tales, too. She learns a great deal about the children through these stories: learns how closely thinking, feeling, and willing are connected at this age of childhood, and how feeling, especially, plays the leading role in all the child's learning experience.

There is no reason why mothers and fathers, as well as teachers, should not make some of these discoveries for themselves by telling fairy tales to their children. It is not the same thing to read to them, for when you are reading, the book separates you from the child. For those who have tried telling these stories but have found it difficult to remember a story, there is a way of learning how. Read the story to yourself as often as you have to, but while reading visualize it as you go along. See the characters, the places, the weather, the action as pictures in your mind's eye. Then, when you start to tell the story, look for these pictures to guide you, and you will find that you can remember.

INTRODUCTION TO NUMBERS

Like other subjects, arithmetic is taught dramatically at a Rudolf Steiner school. Every effort is made to encourage students to experience numbers and arithmetical concepts. The following presentations are examples of how individual teachers have met this challenge by creating stories or exercises or poems relating to numbers.

How the Land Was Divided

Harry Kretz

A story told to the first grade as introduction to the division sign in arithmetic. There was once a king who had two sons. When he became old and weary of his rule he said to his sons, I am old, go and rule my land for me.

Now, it was a very great land, so that part of it lay in the cold, icy north and part lay in the hot, sunny south. When the king was younger, he lived in a castle in the north for a time, and then he lived in another castle in the south for a time. He was the only king who ruled from two castles.

The sons obeyed their father and rode to the castle in the south to rule as their father had done. But there was only one throne, and there was not enough room for both to sit on it, so they quarreled. Besides, the first son did not like the south because he loved the snow and clear, fresh air of the north, so he was doubly unhappy.

Soon the time came for the two sons to go to the castle in the north for a while, to rule the land from the other castle. Here, too, the throne was too small for both to sit on it, and besides, the second son did not like the cold and snow. He loved the hot sun and the green grass.

And so it went on for a long time, until one day the two sons felt that they could not bear their unhappiness any longer. They called a wise old man and told him all about their grief. The wise old man said, You will have a dream and if you can interpret the dream, your sorrows will be ended.

Crayon drawing from a first grade student, arithmetic main lesson

The two sons went to sleep that night, and this is what they dreamed: they were both standing on the bridge that crosses the river that runs across the country exactly halfway between the northern part and the southern part. The first son, who liked the ice and snow and clear fresh air, walked north and sat on the throne in the castle of the north. The second son, who liked the hot sun and green grass, walked south and sat on the throne in the castle of the south. They did not quarrel because there was room for each one on the throne, and they were happy because each one ruled in that part of the land that he liked best. And because they were happy, the people were also happy.

In the morning the two sons woke up and told each other their dream. They had both dreamed the same dream, so they knew that this was the right answer to their question. They were both so pleased with this new way of ruling the land that they told the whole story to every stranger who came to the country.

It was like this, they said. There was a river running straight through the land. There was a castle in the north and in the south—and they drew a picture on the ground like this:

They told the story so often that soon they stopped drawing castles and instead just made two marks to show where the castles stood, and drew a line to show where the river flowed. They said, This is how the land was divided:

Fractions

William Harrer

> *With ordinary numbers we stand on solid ground,*
> *Dealing with whole numbers is fun, so we have found.*
> *But when it comes to fractions it is different indeed,*
> *They are the strangest creatures within the number creed.*
> *In a family of whole numbers you are quite secure,*
> *You see at once when they are tall or small, or rich or poor.*
> *But looking at a fraction, take $\frac{1}{64}$,*

You think it has great value, but what's it really worth?
Compare it with $1/2$; $1/64$ seems tall,
But the truth of the matter is, it is extremely small.
Maybe you'll believe it and maybe you will not,
$1/2$ is 32 times what $1/64$ has got.
If that is not most strange! At least it was for me,
Until I understood the fraction personality.
It is indeed a tragic story when you come to think of it,
Such wholesome numbers as one or two are often sadly split.
Split personalities they have become, oh dear, oh dear,
Divided by a fraction bar they separately appear.
What is above the dividing line we call the numerator,
And that below—strange name indeed—the true denominator.
Which names the fraction, so I'm told,
While the numerator tells how many it shall hold.
Thus fractions that struck me at first with chilling fear,
I seem to grasp with courage now, and they become quite clear.
But how am I to join them in addition or subtraction?
Do fractions, for each other, have any real affection?
When joined both in matrimony a woman gives up her name,
But both fractions in addition have to do the same.
It is easy to determine what the common name should be,
If both fractions come from the same family.
Adding fifth and fifth, you will always have more fifths,
But joining different families, you will have many ifs.
Suppose that Mr. Half joins Miss Third in addition,
They must give up their names to pay for their admission.
Mr. $1/2$ plus Miss $1/3$—now we are in a fix.
Will they be Mr. and Mrs. Half? Oh no, their name is sixth!
Nothing seems common in $1/2$ and $1/3$ to an investigator.
Until he discovers the common denominator.
The 2 in $1/2$ and the 3 in $1/3$ are both factors of six.
And $1/2$ as $3/6$ and $1/3$ as $2/6$ gladly join hands and mix.
Such are but a few of the many complications
In the lives of broken numbers that live in separations.
When we have learned to add some easy fractions

We can part them in like manner when we do subtraction.
But now suppose the halves and thirds join hands in multiplication,
We then have to consider an entirely new implication.
You'd think if they became ⁵/₆ when joining in addition
They'd have to change to many more sixths under this condition.
But no, there is involved a strange complication,
Instead of growing larger, they shrink in this separation.
The numerators multiply each one with all the others,
Completely disregarding their denominator brothers,
Who now stand up together and also claim their right;
While joining hands they multiply in ever friendly spite.
And now you'll come to see in the result of this brave action
The answer is, most strangely, a so much smaller fraction.
The division of fractions is an upside-down affair
About this we could tell you, but it would not be fair
For we fear to tire you with more knowledge of the fractions
When there are in store so many other wholesome actions.
So we want to say just this, and then at last we'll end:
To work with fractions is lots of fun—once you understand.

Why Do We Teach the Norse Myths?

Rudolf Copple

During the tenth year, usually in the fourth grade, a great change begins to operate in the child. Gone is the wonderful confidence of early childhood, of being one with the world. Not in his consciousness, but deep down in his being, the child experiences in an almost physical way: here am I and there is the world, separate from me. This process of inner separation is fraught with two dangers: one, an unhealthy absorption with oneself; the other, being absorbed too much by the world around us. Some children start lying, even consciously, in order to preserve their inner being and also to test this strange world. Others assert themselves more strongly than hitherto; they start to observe, to argue keenly, to become very critical and moody. Suddenly all the children are more aware of differences among people. They want to know whether they are rich or poor, Jewish or Christian; all these things take on a new meaning. Deep questions are hurled at their parents and teachers, and one should take great care to answer them seriously, yet never in a dogmatic way. Although early childhood with its fairy tales and imaginary world is waning or lost forever, their souls are thirsty for meaningful pictures and images filled with inner substance. Their world is not yet one of logical thought, of cause and effect. Every parent and teacher knows that the language of money and its value has no real meaning yet to a ten-year-old. Their point of view is one of likes and dislikes; this is right for their age, and we should not press them into the point of view of adults.

We try to meet these dangers that from now on accompany the life of the child even into adulthood. The curriculum of the Rudolf Steiner schools is built up in such a way that it distinguishes between subjects that loosen the child from the world around him (e.g., history), and subjects in which the surrounding world enters strongly into the child's being (e.g., zoology). During the year the teacher is free to handle these opposites as they best fit the class as a whole. In the fourth grade, however, when the ten-year-old is exposed to these dangers for the first time, there appears a special subject: Norse myths.

It is of course not possible to attempt in the scope of such an article to give a complete picture of the Norse myths. Only a few salient points can be made. The teaching of them carries sublime moments for the children and their teacher.

Just as the child is descending from the heavenly world of childhood, the Norse myths deal with the descent of man from paradise, which they speak of as the twilight of the gods. The possibility for this twilight comes when Loki penetrates into the heavens through the guilt of Odin, the father of the gods. Once there he has three offspring. The first is the Midgard serpent, born out of selfishness. He lives in the sea that surrounds the earth. From there he blows his poisonous breath onto the land until the day of the twilight of the gods, when he will rise and come out of the water onto the land. The second is the wolf Fenris, the animal of the darkening truth and of lies. He will lie in waiting in the woods until the day of the twilight, when he will come forth. The roar coming out of his horrible mouth puts heaven and earth in terror. The third is Hel, who brings sickness and death. The element of evil that penetrates into the heavenly world through Loki represents really the gaining of freedom and egohood of man, the separation from God. With this necessary gift of freedom comes selfishness and untruth into the heart of man. The children are fascinated by the cunning Loki, by his cleverness, yet they detest his immoral deeds, his treachery, and his lack of inner conviction.

In no other mythology is the separation from the heavenly world out of which the children and all of us come, resulting in the loneliness of our egohood, so clearly put in relation to two tempting, assailing forces, the inner world and the outer world, represented by the serpent and Fenris, the wolf. The Old Testament knows of the serpent that lures us in our inner being. The ancient Persians saw the adversary of the outer world in Angra Mainyu. In the Old Testament the fall (i.e., the winning of selfhood) is proved by human guilt. In the Norse myths it is prepared by the gods and comes about through the guilt of a god, Odin. Here the gods themselves know that the descent of egohood (i.e., the full development of man) has to come by their own fall. They themselves lead into it and the twilight. However, with this comes the courage to endure it consciously. The heavenly ego, the image of divine purity and innocence, is given by Baldur the Beautiful. The death of Baldur—of the spirit of childhood, in a way—is brought about by Loki. He manages that Holdur the blind (i.e., blind to the heavenly truth) throws a branch of mistletoe at Baldur, which kills him. Baldur's death is one of the highlights of the whole period. The children are bewildered to the point of crying, for they feel instinctively the truth of this picture. After these happenings the twilight approaches. "Does the twilight come today?" They have a deep curiosity and relationship to this event, yet they also fear it. That the coming of the twilight is mentioned from the moment of Odin's guilt is of the high artistic value to the composition of the stories. The preparation of the inevitable, which brings about a tremendous struggle and the will to overcome the evil at last by the sacrifice of death, is of great moral value. When the terrific battle comes, a hush falls over

Crayon drawing from a fourth grade Norse Mythology main lesson

Mallet from fourth grade woodwork

the class. Although the old gods and their adversaries die, there is a victory by Vidar, a new inner force, really the resurrected ego.

A condensed version of the story goes like this:

The roar of the battle fills the whole world. So formidably surges the howl against the vault of heaven that it bursts and the fiery stars pour down like rain. (In this atomic age is not our foundation in God shaken and broken to pieces?) The wolf Fenris swallows Odin, the creator and father of all. This is his death. Although Thor's hammer crushes the Midgard Serpent, selfishness, the serpent in dying spits poison on Thor, and he sinks down dead. Vidar, however, whose day has finally come, the silent god, who never spoke before the twilight and who represents the new strength of the ego, rises and courageously opposes the wolf, Fenris. With both hands he tears his horrible mouth apart. This is the end of the monster. But now rejoice: Vidar, the son of Odin, is still alive, and in the old stone runes of the gods he can read the name of the new ruler of the heavens and earth. Nobody knows his name, but all have known him since the very beginning.

Thus we can see how the heavenly world comes to an end in the twilight, although there is promise for the future. If we now look at the myths of the creation we can see how the image of man in its fullness is already stated there. In these myths we find two human beings, Askr and Embla, who have just been created out of two trees. They are told to go and look at a mighty tree, the world ash, Yggdrasil, which, translated, means nothing else but the bearer of the ego, the I. From Midgard, their abode, Askr and Embla beheld the world ash, Yggdrasil, which fills the whole world with branches. And the tree started to whisper: Look up at me, I am Yggdrasil. My top gives shade to Asgard, the dwelling of the gods; my crown bears the sun; through my branches circle the moon and stars; in the image of my soul your souls have been formed; look at me and look at yourselves.

And Askr and Embla beheld the tree, half dreaming and half waking by day and night. What did they see?

Three roots they saw. The first went to Niflheim, the frosty, ice-cold land where the realm of death began. In the midst of Niflheim was the fountain of Hvergelmir. Twelve streams came forth from there and ran through the whole world. From where came all the water to the fountain? It dropped down, never stopping, from the antlers of the stag Eik-thrynir, which up in Asgard nibbled at the leaves. Thus it always rained into the fountain.

The second root went to the holy fountain of the Norns. In its water swam singing swans. Ur, Verdandi, and Skuld sat on its shores and let the thread of destiny forever run through their hands.

The third root went to Jotunheim, the realm of the giants. In it was the fountain of Mimir, the wisest being, who could remember all things that had happened.

Every morning the Norns took water out of their fountain and wetted the world ash that its branches might not wither.

High up in the branches of the ash sat an eagle who had a hawk sitting between his eyes. At the fountain Hvergelmir lived the dragon Nithoggr, the hostile, jealous worm. Between the dragon who spat poison and gall against Asgard and the kingly eagle with the hawk was age-old enmity. Ratatoskr, a squirrel, scrambled back and forth day and night up and down the trunk carrying quarrelsome words from the dragon to the eagle and from the eagle to the dragon.

Of all the trees in the world, the world ash, Yggdrasil, suffered most. When the dragon was not quarreling with the eagle, he crawled under the root of the ash where he lived with his offspring and a host of serpents and gnawed on the root with his sharp teeth. Four stags grazed around the ash, biting off its leaves, buds, and branches. Worms and bugs bored into its bark by day and night. Thus decay and death threatened the tree all the time.

Askr and Embla beheld light things and dark things, good things and bad things, noble things and poor things on the tree, and many a secret was revealed to them.

The images here speak a lively language, and if the teacher is aware of what stands behind them, the child will receive a nourishment and help that we could never give him if we told bare facts about human nature that at this age he is unable to grasp or live with. Are not the three roots an image for our thinking, feeling, and willing? The coldness of our thinking pole in Niflheim; the might of our will and also of our lower nature in Jotunheim, and the land of the giants; the region of the heart where our moral convictions live, which form our destiny, depicted in the three Norns weaving the thread of destiny from past to present to future? At the will pole there also lives the dragon, our lower nature. At the thinking pole along with the mighty and noble eagle, which might represent our most noble thoughts, there is the hawk, the vulture whose keen eyes are ever directed downward to the early world, looking for his own advantage, for prey. Is not the scurrying Ratatoskr a beautiful picture of the eternal battle going on between our desires and greed and our ideals and thoughts? Thus the picture of this suffering tree damaged by the stags and bugs is a true image of our ego standing in this world wanting to achieve humanity.

There is a deep significance in all pictures of the Norse myths, and other myths, too, of course, if we are able to read them. It is understood, of course, that only the stories are told to the children, with no interpretation of the images. From these magnificent myths, the child receives the help he needs at his tenth year and the confidence that in spite of all attacks and failures, life is worth living. The teacher can only be deeply grateful that he is allowed to present them, and he can read in the children's faces and in their hearts the help the powerful pictures bring.

WATERCOLOR PAINTING IN THE LOWER SCHOOL

Lucy Schneider

It was a cold January day, but the seventh-grade classroom was hot with the intensity of thirteen-year-old students working their way through a comprehensive physics final test, which included a section on optics—reflection, focal points, virtual and real images. As the students came close to the end of the test and turned to the last page, they looked up at their teacher with ever-widening eyes. "This isn't real!" they cried in disbelief. "It's not for credit, right? I mean, it doesn't count?"

Watercolor from sixth grade geography main lesson

"Everything you do counts," I replied, and gestured to a large white photographer's tray filled with watercolor paper that had been soaking for the last three-quarters of an hour. Beside the tray were pots of cobalt-blue paint diluted with water, paintbrushes, water jars, and a pile of folded paper towels. On the floor alongside this array was a stack of paint boards. The assignment was to paint an illuminated, ice-covered landscape and to include the reflection of the figures in the landscape on the ice.

Although this might seem a frivolous assignment, it was not. It took considerable preparation to assemble the supplies, which were not stored in the classroom since the seventh grade is taught painting by the high school art teacher in the studio. Why then, you might ask, did I choose to do this? To be honest, I saw it as a gift. On a strictly material level, it counted for ten points, which meant that any student who earnestly attempted the assignment would automatically receive ten points on a difficult test. On a soul level, however, I had a very different motive. In our school, seventh grade marks a transition from the lower school years, and in preparation for what is ahead, the students begin to take final tests at the end of main lesson blocks. A bright, lively, and ambitious group, the students had studied for the test. The anxiety level was high, and I intuitively knew that immersing themselves in flowing, translucent color would be healing. There was no need to give directions about how to proceed; after years of painting with their class teacher, the students knew just what to do. Within minutes of settling down to paint, calm descended on the room. The temperature seemed to drop several degrees, and the students were concentrating. No longer calling on information stored in their short-term memories, no longer struggling to articulate concepts that fiendishly eluded their grasp, the students were calling on images that lived in their pictorial imaginations. Hands that had tightly gripped a pencil now lightly held a brush that delicately moved color over gleaming white paper. They were, for the moment, content.

One of the first things a visitor to any Waldorf elementary school will notice is the presence of color. Not the sharp, graphic images of our everyday life but the soft, ambient color that washes the walls of each classroom. Within each room there are large, colorful blackboard drawings created by the teacher to illustrate some aspect of the main lesson, and the bulletin boards are covered with student work—vibrant drawings or paintings. From their very first years, the students work with beeswax crayons to fill empty pages with colorful pictures and words. Gradually, the tools change, the work becomes more refined, but the students continue to confront the blank page and prepare their work with an aesthetic eye.

Third grade watercolor from the farming main lesson

Watercolor painting by a second grade student

Watercolor is an ideal medium for experiencing the creative power of color. The students work with wet paper, liquid paints, and wide brushes. Unlike the dry blocks of watercolor and the tiny brushes that many of us experienced as children, the wet-on-wet method allows for a true exploration of color. The paint spreads and flows freely across the surface of the paper. In the early years, the students work with color stories—yellow spreading its light, blue calmly enclosing, and red boldly charging in—as themes for their paintings. As the students work with these stories, they come to discover what happens when the colors meet each other at the edges or when they overlap to create new colors.

In our school, the first-grade teacher generally works with the three primary colors, and we often work with the translucent pigments, carmine red, cadmium yellow pale, and cobalt blue. The light of the paper shines through the color, creating luminous, clear paintings. At other schools, teachers have begun with a full palette, using denser colors such as vermilion, as well. There are no rules, except that the students gain a valid experience of color.

A question that even the most admiring visitor is likely to ask is why all the watercolor paintings look alike. This is an excellent question. Students are guided through the process of painting a picture by their teacher, who selects images from subjects that have been presented in narrative form in the main lesson. Whether it be a fairy tale or a volcano from a geology main lesson, the teacher is calling upon images that live in the children's imagination. Thus, the word comes first, and then the image.

Watercolor can be like a Mozart piano concerto—clean, precise, every note distinctly audible—or like a Rachmaninoff concerto, where there seem to be more notes than fingers on the hand; some of these notes elude the ear but support the tone quality of the whole. Painting wet-on-wet allows for the freedom to build, change, and move color about the page; it is more like Rachmaninoff. If a color is too strong, the student learns to bring about a balance by strengthening the colors around it rather than trying to take it off the page. If a color is too weak, the student learns how to build it up through adding layers of color. In all cases, the paper has to be prepared and the color has to be built up in such a way that the finished product is not muddy. Some teachers paint with the students; others provide finished paintings to show the students; and still others build the image with colored chalk on the blackboard. Again, there are no rules, except that the students learn how to approach the painting and can work with the security of knowing that there are some parameters and that there is a way to get from the blank page to the image. Over the years, the students learn to refine their brush stroke, and with the knowledge they have gained about color relationships, they strive to bring form to their paintings.

Do all the paintings *really* look alike? The eye, which passively receives images, is actively engaged in the process of painting. The student is constantly observing, judging, and accommodating. Back and forth the active eye moves between the image on the page and the image the teacher has provided, as well as, perhaps unconsciously, the verbal image that lives in the pictorial imagination. The subject matter may be the same, but the variations in each painting are real and distinct, and these differences emerge not only from the particular talents and abilities of each student but also from the particular soul image the student perceives.

The integration of the arts into the curriculum is a distinguishing feature of Waldorf education, and the visual arts are but one component of a vital program that embraces all the arts. Watercolor painting is but one example of our work in this area. Luminous and elegant, watercolor is an extremely challenging medium that requires tremendous discipline. The class teacher develops the student's ability to work successfully with watercolor by presenting the students with verbal images that come directly from the curriculum and by guiding the students through the process with a unifying theme. The word becomes image, and this process deepens the student's relationship to the word.

THE WINGED HORSE: AN ESSAY ON THE ART OF READING

Henry Barnes

Yes, there he sat, on the back of the winged horse! But what a bound did Pegasus make, when, for the first time, he felt the weight of a moral man upon his loins! A bound, indeed! Before he had time to draw a breath, Bellerophon found himself five hundred feet aloft, and still shooting upward, while the winged horse snorted and trembled with terror and anger. Upward he went, up, up, up, until he plunged into the cold misty bosom of a cloud, at which, only a little while before, Bellerophon had been gazing, and fancying it a very pleasant spot. Then again, out of the heart of the cloud, Pegasus shot down like a thunderbolt, as if he meant to dash both himself and his rider headlong against a rock. Then he went through about a thousand of the wildest caprioles that had ever been performed either by a bird or a horse.

Grandfather paused in his reading. The young boy let out a long breath and laughed out loud. What a ride! The old man read on and the boy's eyes shone as he soared in his imagination on the back of the winged horse. His heart beat in rhythm with the powerful sweep of the language and his eyes followed each change of expression on his grandfather's face. He watched the old man's hands twist and flutter and dive as he illustrated how Pegasus soared and plunged on his wild flight.

The boy was just six years old and he was hearing for the first time Hawthorne's wonderful telling of the story of Pegasus and Bellerophon. He asked for the story many times again and often pored over the picture of the winged steed and his young master on the cover of the book.

At the time when he first heard this story, he had not yet entered the first grade, nor could he write his own name. The black printed marks on the white page were mysterious and enchanted forms to him, meaningless and uninteresting in themselves, but from which the grown-ups freed the magic pictures that captured his imagination. And this hidden art the grown-ups called reading.

Each time the story was read aloud, the little boy entered into it as though he heard it for the first time. Pegasus became a familiar companion to him. He saw him rearing in the clouds, and when the sunlight caught the gleaming silver wing of an airplane far up in the blue sky, he cried, "See, there's Pegasus!"

Four or five years later came the great moment when he again discovered this volume of Hawthorne's *Wonder Book* and curled up to read about his beloved Pegasus for the first time himself! And as he read, he once again waited with Bellerophon at the spring and saw Pegasus descend in gleaming spirals from the blue sky and alight on the green grass by the fountain. He did not see the Os and Ss and Bs that his eyes read, for he was far away on the slopes of Mount Helicon. Nowhere did the long words of Latin origin or the difficult Greek names impede his progress, for they were already familiar to his ear and he skimmed over them now, tasting their foreign flavor along with the homely clover of the words he knew.

When had this boy first started to learn to read? It was not in his reading lessons, when he first struggled to spell out words, but when he listened to the stories that were told and read aloud to him, into which he entered with his whole being. For reading is an art—the art of entering with one's whole soul into an experience outside oneself. It is a gleaning of the sunlight hidden in the hard kernel of the word. In its widest meaning, reading is not bound to the printed page, for do we not speak of reading a map? Reading the stars? Reading a man's expression? Reading his mind? It is always an intuitive divining of a meaning that may express itself in as many different ways as there are forms of life: it is always an inner, creative process. The technique of reading the printed word is a specialized branch of the reading process and should no more be confused with it than the technique of raising and lowering the fingers should be confused with the art of a pianist. At a time when in educational circles the art of reading is so generally identified with its mechanics, it is well to remember that many profound minds have been slow readers, often learning to read very late. Many creative writers are poor spellers, and some of the greatest "readers of life" would show up poorly on the current reading tests designed to show "intelligence"!

A vast amount of research has been done on the technique of reading and there now exists such a literature on "reading" that one who conscientiously tries to master it all is not likely to have either the courage or the time to attempt to teach children to read, or to read anything interesting himself! Much valuable and important knowledge has been gained, but the essence of how we learn to read remains, I believe, a mystery. That is, it is a living process, like learning to swim or to play the violin, which can only be grasped by doing it and can never be fully analyzed intellectually or reduced to merely mechanical principles. Every good swimming teacher knows that the key to success is to let the beginner discover that he cannot sink if he tries. Water is buoyant, and the first thing is to establish this confidence and let the learner enjoy this friendly element. And so also in learning to read, the key to success is the love and enjoyment of the great stories and poems that are the element in which the reader swims. Before a printed reader is ever opened, we must have done everything in our power to strengthen the inner muscles of the imagination and to awaken a love and enthusiasm for the living literature that the child is to read.

It is for this reason in a Rudolf Steiner school that reading does not begin until the letters have been developed out of pictures and until the child has been steeped in the hearing, retelling, and acting out of the stories that he will later read. Toward the end of the first grade, two or three of the favorite stories are condensed into a few short sentences, these are written down, and each child has thus made his own first reader! Only then does he meet these same stories again in a printed book.

Learning new words, practicing word families, sounding out the syllables, all of this necessary work belongs in special lessons that parallel the reading lessons but are not allowed to destroy the germinating, imaginative process of the reading itself.

What, then, makes a good reader for young children? Is it the scientifically streamlined text that tells an obvious story in words of one syllable, adding a measured dose of new words in each chapter? Is this the way life chooses? If so, we should speak a "graded speech" in the presence of our young instead of exposing them to the full richness of adult language, which is the matrix out of which, by imitation, their individual language grows. No!

Let us turn again to one of our great American educators, who never taught school but who wrote some of the living stories that have educated us all. Nathaniel Hawthorne, in 1851, wrote in the introduction to his *Wonder Book and Tanglewood Tales:*

> In performing this pleasant task,—for it has been really a task fit for hot weather, and one of the most agreeable, of a literary kind, which he ever undertook,—the author has not always thought it necessary to write downward in order to meet the comprehension of children. He has generally suffered the theme to soar, whenever such was its tendency, and when he himself was buoyant enough to follow without effort. Children possess an unestimated sensibility to whatever is deep or high, in imagination or feeling, so long as it is simple, likewise. It is only the artificial and the complex that bewilders them.

It is not the poverty-stricken renderings of obvious and ordinary events that we should give children as their first experiences of reading. Let us have the courage to do what our forefathers did when they gave fairy tales, and poems, told by the masters of language. Let us avoid what is artificial and complex. If the imagination that created the pictures of the fairy tales is deep and pure and if the thought underlying them is clear and true, then, with the right guidance, the difficulties of vocabulary will prove no stumbling block and the beauty of the language will itself prove a most potent educational force. Let us have confidence in the buoyancy of language, as we do in water, for language is one of the great creative powers of the race. And let us not fail to value the educative power of what is half understood in what the children read. This strange word, often beautiful in its sounds, placed like an emerald in its native rock, stirs the imagination and allows the child's soul to surmise a shadowy world that it will one day understand but that now is veiled in mystery. Isn't this reaching out to grasp what cannot yet be fully understood an important part of every growth?

The question may very naturally arise: should children read and hear stories and poems that tell of tragedy or present some gruesome and fearful incident? Is the death of Christ on the Cross or the devouring of Red Riding Hood's grandmother by the wolf fit matter for a child of five, six, or seven, or eight? Doesn't the answer depend on another question: *how* is the incident told? Is it presented realistically, physically? Or is it presented artistically, so that it is a fact grasped by the imagination, like a picture in a dream? Experience usually shows that it is the realistic fact that shocks and frightens a child, whereas the same boy or girl may cheerfully digest Red Riding Hood's grandmother, the

Crayon drawing from a first grade language arts main lesson

six little kids, and many other delectable morsels when the presentation is true to the spirit of the fairy tale. Here again, it is life that should be allowed to speak and life is woven of good and evil—of love and hate—and it is life alone that can educate for life.

A child cannot understand the meaning of the Crucifixion, but when he reads, or hears, the quaint old folk legend of Robin Redbreast,* which tells how a little bird sat on the edge of its nest, grieving, as it watched the bowed head of Jesus upon the Cross, a picture is planted, like a seed, in his heart that will grow as the child grows. With the little bird, the child says, "No one comes to soothe His pain. So I will try to comfort Him." And whenever he watches a fat robin, plucking at insects in the grass, the child will remember how the legend tells that the little bird flew to the Cross and was able to pull a thorn out of the Savior's head, and how at the same time a drop of blood fell upon the bird's nest. And Jesus' words: "As an eternal reminder, dear Bird, thou and thy family shall carry this red spot on your breasts and men shall call thee Robin Redbreast," will echo in his childish heart with a tender joy. Understanding for the event on Golgotha will blossom later, but it will be nourished from the half-remembered soil of this early experience. And a whole lifetime is not too long to understand life's central mysteries.

No writers ever spoke more directly to the hearts of young children than the brothers Grimm, and their *Household Tales* must rank among the great educational books of all time. It is interesting to hear what they had to say on this question, in 1819, in their Preface to the *Tales*:

> Should one nevertheless object that one thing or another causes embarrassment to parents and is objectionable to them, so that they even do not wish to place this book in their children's hands, this anxiety may in single cases be justified, and they may easily make a selection; on the whole, that is for a healthy condition, this is certainly unnecessary. Nothing can defend us better than nature herself, which allowed these blossoms and leaves to grow up in this color and form; for whom they are unacceptable according to his special purposes he can not demand that they should therefore be otherwise colored or cut to shape. One might also say, rain and dew fall as a blessing upon everything which grows on earth; he who does not dare to set out his plants because they are too delicate and might be harmed, and waters them rather with tepid water in his room, will not therefore demand that there should be no rain or dew. Everything can flourish which is natural, and this is what we want to keep in mind. What is more, we know no healthy and vigorous book, which has educated the people, with the Bible in first place, where such reservations do not apply in still greater degree; the right usage does not find evil in them, but rather, as a beautiful proverb says, a testimony of our hearts.

* *The Golden Footprints and Other Fairy Tales* (Adonis Press, 1949).

Since the beginnings of a written language, reading has never been the problem that it is considered to be today. It will not cease to be a problem so long as the technique of reading is regarded as an end and not as a means. It is the instrument of a great art, of which the reading of the printed word is a specialized and highly abstract part. Let us have the courage to teach the art and we will find that the nightmare of "reading difficulties" and its attendant train of "remedial reading" practices are not as inevitable and frightening as they appear to be. Our children's bodies will grow strong if we feed them natural, healthy foods. Their souls will grow strong on a diet of the truly great, imaginative literature of the human race.

Phonetics, word associations, sentence structure, and all the techniques of good reading must be taught and drilled, but do not let us confuse these with reading. As teachers, let us learn how to prepare our reading lessons so that they serve to stir and strengthen the wings of the imagination, which may help our children to read the reality of life when they enter it as adult human beings.

Speech and Poetry in the Lower School

Christy Barnes

What a great delight it is to hear a clear voice, warm with enthusiasm, and firm with the power of well-directed thought! There is little that so quickly inspires our confidence as this, for speech expresses the activity of the nature behind it. It has been said that the style is the man, and it is equally true to say that speech is the man. Impediments such as stuttering and lisping are the most obvious indications of psychological difficulties. But if the ear be sufficiently awake, it also can distinguish subtle shades of character and temperament through the tone of voice, through the clarity or clumsiness with which the individual sounds are formed, and through the flow or hesitation of spoken sentences. It is a book by means of which one may learn to read man's nature.

Listen to human speech as it develops from babyhood onward. The vowels of tiny children still sing like bird notes in the air and scarce seem yet embodied. We may learn from them the art of keeping speech musical. A baby's precise little *t* and upwelling *l* may teach us their fineness. When they enter school, children love harmonious poems that still have a certain dreamy element, poems full of nature, picture, and sound. One senses that poems should bubble, rush, skip, and flow rhythmically but never move in a mechanical beat. *Shh! sss, ff, bzz*—every sound describes and dramatizes a world of immense busy-ness, mystery, and importance. Every word is uttered out of their whole being. As boys and girls grow a little older, they delight in tongue twisters. At ten they are ready to roll out a rousing sea song, laugh through a jolly poem, and follow the stealthy steps of a verse that pursues the prowling tiger through the jungle. On the other hand, there are children who show in vague articulation or in high-pitched, ineffectual tones that they are not penetrating into their own bodies or into life as one would expect. Still others gasp nervously and repeat sentences in a jerky manner to an accompaniment of excited gestures of head and hands.

In the early teens, when they begin to war within themselves, the children feel a need for poems and plays of an especially dramatic character: tragic Scottish ballads, heroic sagas, or good full-hearted comedies. But it is also at this age that some of the children take on one predominant manner of speaking. This may even develop later into a veritable caricature of human speech in which one element of soul—feeling, will, or intellect—develops out of all proportion to the others. Such is the case with the voice of the bombastic orator that swells in unctuous curves and betrays him every moment as insincere and self-engrossed; the rasping bark of a rude official; or again the dry voice of a pedant, so boring that it makes the listener squirm like a small schoolboy on his chair. It is indeed disheartening to hear in the voice of a fourteen-year-old that, for him, the world is already a finished book and that the openness and freshness of childhood lies behind him. Yet today something of this quality does creep now and then into the voices of children.

Quite foreign elements may also penetrate into their speech. Many of us have become inured to them and no longer notice. Our ears have grown callous today. The stridency, nervousness, and poverty of much of the speech around us go unobserved; and so the din and tenseness of the city steal into our voices unawares. We forget the discrepancy between the human voice and the tones that come over the radio and in the movies. Yet even in the finest of mechanical instruments the metallic material makes this difference inevitable. Moreover, it is infectious. Some children imitate this metallic quality with nasal or throaty speech, and one senses that a hardening or coarsening process is taking place within them.

How can we work against these tendencies? How can we help the children to develop the hearty, clear, and mobile speech that at the same time works so deeply into the soul and body as to establish health, confidence, and vitality? Rudolf Steiner, in his many lectures on drama, poetry, and speech, has shown how poetry and drama—the most creative forms of speech—are in turn the creative forces that heal and revivify the speech organs themselves. He tells how the true forces of speech demand the response of the whole human being, not merely of one soul power such as the intellect.

Speech is so intimately connected with our entire nature that it reflects both difficulties and developments. In speech the inner being stands before us audibly, so to say, and it is then possible to work back upon the inner nature through this audible medium. One can experience at least a small evidence of this possibility by assuming a new voice—and finding how, for a moment, one becomes a new person. If we act the confidence we have not and act the part well, the confidence itself is established. This is quite as true of other human powers. One may even reawaken the fresh powers and wholeheartedness of childhood that are apt to fade away so early today. In this way speech becomes a healing and balancing as well as an artistic activity.

One has a visible proof of this fact as one stands before a group of children who are about to recite a poem in chorus. The enthusiasm of the moment awakens the dreamy children from the top of their heads to the soles of their feet. The shy ones, feeling themselves hidden within the group, are relieved of self-consciousness and learn to speak out fully and naturally. The mischief-makers become leaders who pour their energy into the most dramatic parts of the poem. One can see in the children's eyes and even in the color of their cheeks how the speaking of rhythms, which have sprung from a great imagination, harmonizes and strengthens the breath and pulse! How it actually invigorates the lungs and circulation. Rudolf Steiner has indicated the natural connection between poetic rhythms and the varying relations of breath and pulse beat. It is even true that under the direction of a teacher with the proper knowledge, stuttering and asthma may be cured by repeated recitation of certain harmonizing rhythms.

It takes time and patience to train the speech of an older person, but the larynx of a child is soft and pliable, his articulation and breathing are still easily influenced. Those children are fortunate indeed who have the opportunity to imitate a fine, vigorous, and supple speech. The kind of speech they hear every day is of the greatest importance to children. Either it helps to build capacities or it lays the foundation for future impediments. The ear, which is an integral part of the speech organism, transmits its impressions directly to the larynx and the larynx vibrates in harmony with these impressions. It is thus constantly being molded by all the sounds the child hears about him. Later the organism will become harder and will respond less subtly to what it hears.

This is why it is invaluable for a child to learn a foreign language at an early age. He will acquire an excellent accent in a short time. He may forget many of the words he learns, but the capacity for a good accent has been established. Even should the language itself never be of practical use to him, the effect of learning it has been practical in the deepest sense, for it has given a mobility to the speech organs and a scope of experience to the soul, which will remain with him.

The natural way for children to learn poetry is through the ear. It becomes alive to them when they use the vowels and consonants as the painter uses his colors and the dancer his gestures. They re-create fire and fury with flaming *f*s, send the snake slithering through the grass with a hissing *s*, paint the rushing and ripple of water with its own sounds, and make a sword cut with a strong, clear *k*. In this way the sounds themselves urge on the tongue and lips to form them agilely and clearly, and poetry again helps to form and refine the speech organism. The result is not the affected and static speech that the teaching of elocution sometimes brings about, but a natural command and enjoyment of the sounds. If the children have practiced the eurythmic gestures for each different sound, they will have an especially living sense of the descriptive power of language.

All children love poetry when it is given its full expression. They only find it deadly dull when it has been maimed in some way, when someone has deprived it of its vitality, ironed out the dancing motion of its rhythms, or leveled down the greatness of its imagination. Then only a skeleton remains.

It is the living being that interests children, and if they are allowed to help embody this being they can never forget it, much less dislike it. They will remember it with a certainty quite different from the hesitating stammer so often the result of laborious memorizing through the eye. And it is the greatest poetry that they love best: Shakespeare, Shelley, Blake. Even if they do not grasp the meaning intellectually, they will carry with them the pictures, sounds, and noble rhythms as creative impulses for their whole lives.

If children have plunged into the element of speech as heartily as this, their voices will escape the prevailing rigid and didactic tones. They will bring form into their speech and escape the influences which would coarsen or make it nervous. Poetry and drama never allow the soul to become passive or static. And if from an early age a child has lived with these, then the soul and the voice will remain pliable and eager for new and ever-changing experience.

THE IMPORTANCE OF HANDIWORK
IN THE WALDORF SCHOOL

Patricia Livingston

The hands are a unique and beautiful part of the human being, and they bring us important, far-reaching experiences. Therefore, as teachers we must try to help the children become aware of their hands and of the great gifts they bestow on themselves and on others. Their hands need to become skillful, sensitive, and strong so that they can accomplish many wonderful deeds. Blind people get to know the world through their hands, but most people are unaware of the knowledge that can be gained when they are used in sensitive and useful ways. Think of art and music! Think of what physical work and daily tasks teach us. Think of a handshake and what it tells us about another person.

Handwork and crafts should be imaginatively and artistically taught, so that the children are encouraged to make original designs that are colorful and creative in form. The children should learn new ways to use color and make designs that indicate the practical use of the project. Rudolf Steiner gave several indications of how this can be done. The

Knitted pig by a second grade student

painting and form drawing the children do in all their lessons are extremely important. Working with color and experiencing how colors flow into one another in painting affects everything they do in and beyond handwork lessons, fostering artistic, imaginative growth in their thinking as well.

We want the children to make things they love and enjoy, to work skillfully, always increasing their artistry. Handwork should be relaxing and fun, and at the same time productive, involving strong will activity. Nothing happens if you don't use your hands and get to work! Working to transform the materials of the earth fosters inner growth and a sense of well-being in the children. These lessons support and complement other subjects in the school, helping to bring balance and wholeness to the education.

In the mature artist, handwork and crafts become a balanced activity of thinking, feeling, and willing. The *will* is the part of us that is most asleep. Handwork can gently wake up and educate the will, starting at an early age. Why is this so important?

The will is ultimately connected to the thinking. It is really the task of every Waldorf teacher to help the children become clear, imaginative thinkers, human beings who can go into any profession or any area of work with new, creative ideas—ideas that will be urgently needed as we meet the twenty-first century. The whole Waldorf curriculum guides the children in this direction, beginning in the kindergarten, where the creative play of the young child stimulates the inner forces that later become active in the creative thinking of the adult.

Cross stitch pillows by fourth grade students

Through beauty, color, and form, handwork and crafts help to lead the children from play to imaginative thinking as adults, forming a kind of bridge between the two. The hands play an important part in this awakening. The activity of the fingers stirs the senses that connect the child to the world, and his whole life of thought begins to move.

Handwork and crafts have been taught in all the grades since the beginning of the first Waldorf school. Rudolf Steiner wanted the boys and girls to work together in these classes. In this he was way ahead of his time! It was unheard of to have boys doing handwork in 1919! Why did he insist on this radical change? Because, he said, these activities led to the enhancement of judgment. Judgment comes out of the imaginative forces, working through the heart. It is not the head alone but the whole human being that forms a judgment. Think how many of the senses are used in handwork—sight, touch, movement, balance, and many others. The senses take in different impressions of the world and join them together to form a judgment. Our hands bring us into a deeper, closer relationship to the world and, therefore, to a greater understanding of humanity.

Much of handwork has to do with waking up, seeing things, and noticing details. Recent brain research has found that using the hands opens up neurological pathways that would otherwise atrophy. In other words, the interrelationship of the hand and eye working together allows more neurological pathways to function. So one could say that handwork with young children is a training ground for thinking, and the more one includes the cultivation of beauty and feeling, the more creative will the intellectual thinking become.

Many things are happening simultaneously in the handwork classes. First, of course, one wants the children to learn practical skills, to learn how to use the tools, to respect and care for the tools and other materials involved, and also to form ideas about what they wish to make, creating their own designs, and then actually bringing to completion a beautiful, well-made project. It is a most satisfying experience to make something and see the practical results. This is true confidence building. Therefore, we must see to it that all the projects the children make are things they can learn to do by themselves, that there are no hidden steps done by the teacher, and that the work is finished on time.

Some children need more help and encouragement than others in order to achieve such goals, but the wise teacher will know how to guide them without destroying their confidence and sense of achievement. Confidence in one subject is carried over into another. Activating the will through handwork strengthens ability in all subjects.

There are immense therapeutic possibilities in handwork teaching. Waldorf teachers must study and strive to understand Rudolf Steiner's view of the developing child—an ongoing work for all of us. One must learn to work age-appropriately and to study the

Socks knit by a fifth grade student
Scarf and needles created by a first grade student

different types of children—small- and large-headed, and the like—and it is essential to try to understand and work with the temperaments. We must know the children so well that we begin to see exactly what each child needs. How much help will move someone forward? Who needs to slow down and perhaps redo work that is poorly and thought-lessly done? How do you handle a melancholic perfectionist? With the older children it is important that they begin to develop some self-awareness in these areas.

Resourcefulness is developed as the children see how much they can achieve starting with a few simple materials. Many simple tasks are no longer experienced in the home. Children today often have no idea of how to sew on a button! When a child learns the "magic trick" of putting a cord in a drawstring bag, he is thrilled! He then becomes more interested and resourceful in solving other problems.

The gifts of nature fill our handwork lessons and create an opportunity to involve the children in the world of ecology and social interaction. The children experience wool, cotton, and many other fibers through using them. They learn of their sources and about natural dyes for colors, and how humanity has contributed to their use. Respect and reverence are fostered for all we receive and for how mankind and nature work together. We should use only natural fibers in our classes, if possible. To touch silk or wool is a very different experience from that of handling synthetic materials. Our Waldorf kindergarten children know that well!

In a first grade, as we use our beautiful wool, we talk about the sheep. If you go to the Rudolf Steiner School in Great Barrington, you probably pass the sheep farm daily. The children see the sheep gradually grow heavy with wool, and then suddenly, one day, they see them shorn—a rather shocking experience. So we discuss how generously the sheep give their wool for our scarves and also talk about the craftsmen who spin it into yarn for us. First-grade children know from the fairy tales how "magical" spinning is and still retain a feeling of wonder about spinning straw into gold. We also speak about the trees from which our wooden needles are made. The children learn to value and not waste these gifts. Conversations such as these continue into the upper grades, changing according to the ages and to what materials they are using and what crafts they are learning. At the appropriate time modern technology will also be discussed.

All this helps the children make a real connection to their surroundings, closing a gap created by a modern world in which everything appears out of stores in a somewhat abstract way, made out of unimaginable materials that seem worthless and easily disposable. The children see so much waste! Through the handwork classes they gain a realistic knowledge of, and a reverence for, the world of nature and become aware of ecological problems that arise in our modern world. We need to encourage new perspectives and foster a real social consciousness.

THE MUSIC CURRICULUM

George Rose

Today music is taught in most schools. Great numbers of dedicated music teachers work with enthusiasm for the benefit of their students. If one were to inquire why music is taught, many reasons would be given, primary among them being that music brings happiness into children's lives, it harmonizes children, and it provides an artistic balance to intellectual subjects. All of this is true, and the music curriculum in a Waldorf school achieves these aims. Yet one hopes we achieve much more, for through music we can participate in the development of the growing child.

Every child is born with an innate musicality. Since the purpose of Waldorf education is to preserve and strengthen all that the child bears within himself when coming into the world, music should play an important role in his education. The means by which a child will do his own unique task must be created by a strengthening of the child's will. A strong music program can help him go forth in life and meet its challenges with enthusiasm and confidence.

At the Waldorf school in which I teach, music permeates the school and the community. The lives of everyone connected with the school are in some way touched by music. From the preschool years, when singing and rhythmic activities abound, through the middle school years, when all children have singing and orchestral work, until the high school years, when the entire school sings as a chorus, and the orchestra is selective, music pervades the school and helps make it the healthy school it is.

The music curriculum at this Waldorf school has developed from, and within, the philosophy of the school, and is aimed at strengthening the will of the child. Making music demands that a person's entire being be present at the moment of execution. To sing well, or to perform well, demands an active will. I can think of no other activity that so involves the powers of thinking, feeling, and, in particular, willing than making music does, for the manual and vocal skill it demands is a result of concentrated thinking, and intensified feeling, both translated into action.

We try to help children define and bring to consciousness the music they are born with. Our instruction is aimed not only at unfolding each child's musical talents but also at developing his human qualities, since music will harmonize and lift the inner nature of the child. In seeking to achieve these aims, we educate each child to enjoy music, to read music, and to perform music.

In our lower school, as at other Waldorf schools, each child experiences daily recorder playing with his class teacher. This begins in the first grade and continues throughout the child's lower school years, depending on the ability of the class teacher. By beginning with the recorder and singing, leading to orchestral instrument playing, we hope to aid the school's development of the child's will.

First Grade. We spend one hour and thirty-five minutes a week on singing and rhythm. The unison singing involves simple melodies, which are usually pentatonic. Work is done with matching tones, usually within the range of the fifth. The child experiences much movement to music through walking, running, skipping, and clapping. We use some percussive instruments in the hope that the child will discover the differences between rhythm and beat. Often the class participates in singing circle games.

Second Grade. We use one hour and forty-five minutes a week to develop all techniques used in the first grade and to develop new musical ideas. Here we introduce rounds and canons in singing, in speech, and with rhythm instruments. We do some work with simple part songs and introduce the tone ladder, a wooden staff made for us by the shop teacher, upon which the child places the tones, or notes. Melodies within the range of the octave are taught, often with scale numbers. Sometimes we introduce singing books that contain only the words, but only with songs the children already know. We also do simple folk dances with the circle.

Third Grade. Each week we use two hours and thirty minutes to develop the musical techniques used in the first and second grades. In this class the children are introduced to more involved part songs and canons. They begin to read notes and to write on the staff. Now they are ready to invent melodies and to experiment with the conductor's beat. They also learn more complicated dances and dance in lines with changing partners.

Fourth Grade. Two hours and thirty minutes are given each week to the study of music in this year. Each child begins an orchestral instrument. We ask parents to provide private lessons; the school's Music Fund helps pay for lessons for those who cannot. The class meets twice a week for orchestra. The first part of the year is devoted to playing two parts on the recorder. We make serious attempts to read music from the staff, and when the class seems to be reading music from the staff with the recorder, we begin orchestra. Sometimes this is in November, but it has been as late as March. The student chooses an instrument, usually one the teacher has suggested, and begins lessons. The orchestra time is spent reading music from orchestra books. In the one singing period a week we make an effort to do part songs in 3/4 and 4/4 time.

Fifth Grade. We divide two hours and forty minutes a week between orchestra and singing. In orchestra we continue the techniques used in the fourth grade, but with more difficult music. In singing we work on unison and two- and three-part songs. Rhythmic work continues. Preliminary work begins with music theory—intervals, major keys, and scales. The children continue to conduct songs, and to conduct each other in singing.

Sixth Grade. Again, we divide two hours and forty minutes a week among orchestra, singing, and music theory. In orchestra we continue the work done in the fourth and fifth grades. In singing, we try to awaken musical judgment. We begin to study theory and form and introduce the circle of fifths. The students continue to work with major scales and keys and begin to work with minor scales and keys. They study intervals and write music with choral structure and melody. They sing in two and three parts and listen to records of serious music.

Seventh and Eighth Grades. One hour and fifty minutes of music is required each week, and one hour and ten minutes of music is optional. Orchestra is the optional music group. Those who continue (and this is usually most of the class) work on more advanced music. We sing two- and three-part music and begin the study of voice training; often we talk of the theory of music, and sometimes introduce a listening lesson. Sometimes we ask the groups to write music. It is vital that some singing periods be divided between boys and girls.

High School. We hope that all of the music work done in grades one through eight can come to fruition in the high school. Here chorus is required one forty-five-minute period a week. During the present school year the Christmas section of Handel's *Messiah* was prepared and performed with student and graduate soloists and a graduate orchestra. A Gilbert and Sullivan operetta, presented biannually, is also prepared during this period. The high school orchestra meets for forty-five minutes twice a week, and performs at school assemblies and community affairs such as the Adelphi University graduation. In the orchestra we attempt to teach the great literature in music, but that depends on the instrumentation available, and it fluctuates yearly. The Waldorf Singers, a special chorus of approximately forty students, has become a very well known performing group, having sung throughout the East, and having made a European tour in 1971, appearing at many Waldorf schools. This group, following the tradition of all a cappella choirs, is taught to sing music spanning five centuries. During the eleventh-grade year, a three-week block of history of music becomes part of the study of history.

On the graduate level the Waldorf Institute of Liberal Education has two three-week blocks of the study of music in its schedule. During this time, methods of teaching music are studied, as well as work with voice placement and singing. This group plays recorder throughout the year.

The Waldorf Choral Society is a dues-paying group of approximately ninety adults dedicated to the study of the great choral masterworks. This group meets each Monday night for two hours. Included in the Choral Society are Waldorf school teachers, parents, and graduates. High school juniors and seniors are eligible to sing. The annual Baroque Festival presented by the Choral Society has become a musical highlight in the school and on Long Island.

The Waldorf Artists Series was born in 1976 when the school's music department received a foundation grant. Artists such as Stanley Drucker, clarinetist, and Bernard Krainis, recorder player, have appeared on this series, as well as the New Hungarian Quartet, the Philador Trio, and the Rascher Saxophone Quartet.

This same foundation grant has made possible the acquisition of many orchestral instruments and has aided the Music Fund, which annually pays for lessons for approximately a dozen students.

It is fundamental to the Waldorf School philosophy that the whole is greater than its parts only when attention and care are given to details. A Waldorf school should be permeated by music, and a music curriculum should be formed by great attention to ways in which this art can help the child. Rudolf Steiner stated, "Waldorf education . . . aims to raise children who are strong and sound in body, free in soul, and lucid in spirit." Music, once it becomes a part of the child's inner self, will resound in him and help him to be free through his life. It will work upon his being and live in his memory. As with other forces developed in childhood, it will remain with him forever.

EURYTHMY

Kari Van Oordt

1

Here comes the fourth grade! Yes, like all fourth-grades: noisy and lively, everybody talking at the same time, pushing each other, laughing and scolding, boisterous and careless. Steer them directly into the rhythm of the anapest—

On the winds, over wave,
On the clouds, over dale,
Over hills, over vale,
Over treetops and trail . . .

and let them sweep off the overflow of uncontrolled activity; bring them into a form that will hold them and strengthen their individual control. It takes a while to form the circle well, for everyone has to make an active effort to give it the perfect roundness of the ideal circle. If the form is sloppily built, it will impress sloppiness into the child. If the form is strong and firmly built, it will impress the child with inner strength.

Eurythmy is movement, form, and content:
Movement in rhythm, in breathing life,
Form in control and action,
Content through the image-making thought power.

The circle is the thought content in this case, formed by controlled action. When this form is alive, there is an inner flow of movement through all the shoulders, forming the circle line.

And now they proceed into outer movement: let the circle expand, let it contract, expand, contract, the circle begins to breathe. Now the single child loosens from the circle and swings into a rhythmic contracting and expanding. Watch how they bend forward with close, tight arms to contract, then to expand into a far-reaching stretch across the

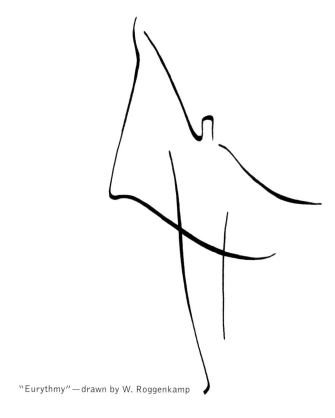

"Eurythmy" — drawn by W. Roggenkamp

room. Here you see the invigorating rhythm of the iambic, the "short-long," ᴗ- , and in doing this the children enter a disciplined activity of controlled movement. They come into shape and are ready to get down to work.

Another day, or in another grade, you might need another kind of rhythm to bring them into readiness. You might choose the rhythm of trochee, the -ᴗ , what can be called a "falling" rhythm. It brings you down, in a calming way, down into yourself with the long beat, the expansion, and lets the contraction hold you back in the short, preventing the long from pulling you too deeply down.

The whole child comes to expression in these movements with the rhythmic breathing. The soul contracts and expands with the bending and stretching and is strengthened in its balance between the inner soul life and the body.

It is the task of education to guide the child in seeking this balance. The key to the guidance, at the age of the elementary school child, is rhythm. It is in the rhythmic system, in the realm of feeling, that the child can live and experience in this period of his development. Watch how he listens to a story, or how he jumps down the stairs or on the paved sidewalk.

Everything the class teacher does is formed out of the element of rhythm, whether it is the way he changes from the activity of writing to that of reading, or the change from singing to listening, from one subject to the other. Rhythm arises in the change from one thing to the other: short—long, in—out, day—night. Observe the rhythmic way he hands out the crayons, or the way he tells a story, or leads them into arithmetic. For the children learn their tables by stamping their feet as they walk about and clap their hands:

uu- 1,2,3—4,5,6,—7,8,9—10,11,12

or when they learn the letters and step rhythmically their "letter verses":

The king is kind and never cruel,
And that is why the king can rule.

Or any rhythmic nursery rhyme:

Ride, ride, my hobblediho,
Back and forth my rockers go.

If at a particular moment the children need to wake up in their feet and legs, they might run this little rhythm, neatly and fast on their tiptoes (starting with the whole foot):

Hey-ho, let the wind blow.
Let the frost glitter and let the rain flow.
Primulas peeping and scillas done sleeping
And daffodils keeping the borders aglow.

We have an endless variety of rhythmic stepping or running, and the teacher will choose, out of his pedagogical insight, just the kind of rhythm the child needs at that particular moment. A refreshing anapest, uu- , or iambic, u- , quieting dactyl, -uu , or trochee, -u , for each rhythm has a different effect upon the child.

When we make use of rhythm in this manner, we take the rhythmic element into the arms and legs, into the action of the will, and we have the most wonderful varieties for our rhythmic classroom exercises.

In dealing with eurythmy itself, however, in the eurythmy lesson, we center the rhythmic activity in the rhythmic system, in the chest, where the heartbeat and the contracting-expanding lungs are situated. Our feelings live and come to expression in our heartbeat and rhythmic breathing, as our thinking lives in our head, and our will expresses itself in the action of our arms and legs. Centered in the rhythmic system, we let the movement flow into the realm of the will and that of thinking, emphasizing the breathing in the movement. Breathing in—breathing out. Make a large out-breathing gesture on the whole line of this simple verse of the Hopi Indians: "Far as man can see"; and then in-breathing on the next: "Comes the rain, comes the rain to me"; out-breathing gesture: "From the Rainmount, Rainmount far away"; in: "Comes the rain, comes the rain to me." Try the same with single syllables, not by stepping with the feet, but as contracting and expanding movement of the whole body, far stretched across the room:

The moon is up, the stars are bright,
The wind is fresh and free.

as a contrast to the falling rhythm of the evening verse:

Now the day is over,
Night is drawing nigh,

where the short comes after the long.

We have many different ways we can let the children move with these breathing rhythms. Some rhythms emphasize more the thinking quality of the breathing: "The rose is a rose and was always a rose," and others will go strongly into the dramatic breathing of action: "Wild are the winds of winter, when furiously forth they fly." In this way the entire child is actively involved while giving form and control to the rhythmic motion.

This kind of controlling content, form, and rhythm is like learning to control life itself. It does not make sense to do a eurythmy movement while you are thinking of other things, or while your thoughts wander about. The thought has to go into the movement and penetrate the body that forms it. That makes the movement a totally conscious one. The whole body is being penetrated with thought and feeling and will.

A mastery of the body can be observed in the child's development.

2

In the eurythmy lesson of the first grade the children are absorbed in the fairy-tale imagination and follow the teacher into the pictures of dramatic action and suspense. They move in an atmosphere of wonder. In both the first and second grades the children enter into the mood created in the lesson and live imitatingly in the movement of the teacher (and woe to the child if the teacher's movement has any kind of tension or disharmony—it is all being reflected in the children!). The second-grader still moves in the mood of wonder and imitation, but the gestures are done more knowingly.

In the third grade the children grow somewhat more independent. They can reach out, although still in a dreamlike state of mind, with arm movements extending into the loft realms where the Bible stories come from, and at other times with their feet closer to the ground where their house building takes place. (Bible stories fit exactly into the eurythmy ability at that point in the third grade, when the children have an all-embracing joy of movement).

The fourth grade is a time of waking up, full of restless and jerky movements. The children are helped by running a square across the room, with firm steps and controlled shoulders. Let them cross with each other in two straight lines, just like the cross-stitch they are doing in their handwork lesson, and they will be helped to wake up in the right way, to free and controlled actions.

As the fifth-grader, with his body movement, seems to peep somewhat curiously into the adulthood of life, he develops in eurythmy a stretch and bend of the body that may be of great beauty and lightness, the last joyous lightness of body before entering the sixth grade, where the children seem to get heavy so fast! Heavy, sloppy, and lazy! The main lesson curriculum asks for Roman history, focused on law and order! Geometry with precision. Yes, of course, that is exactly what the sixth-graders need in movement, in order to gain control over their action and thinking. They move a great deal in geometric forms and struggle to make the shape exact and clear; they move to music pieces, trying to catch the pure tones in melody and rhythm. If they can master these things, they can display a harmonious radiance as at no other age.

The seventh-grade eurythmy lesson brings music and poems where the children can learn to enter a controlled forming of the various moods of soul. This gives them real satisfaction for their disquieted state of body and soul at this age.

The eighth grade is like an octave in the field of music. Having gone through the seven grades in eurythmy with the form element gradually developing from simple to more and more complicated, they should now have themselves in hand and be able to move in group formations, which require both skill and dramatic expression as well as cooperation with the movement of their fellow students. Take a simple form, with twelve people moving together, in three different rhythms. It cannot be done unless each of the twelve is keenly aware of one another's movement. At this age we also work a great deal with contrasts, to stay flexible in our thinking and controlled in our expansion and contraction.

Eurythmy exercise

When we come to the high school we meet young girls and boys, students, not children anymore. In eurythmy we stand upright with a different consciousness. In kindergarten, when we stood upright, we lived in the imagination of being a tall tree; now, in high school, we stand upright as a thinking human being. The straight and curved lines we ran along joyously with our legs in the first grade are now being formed and modeled in space with the movement of the body, everything more knowingly now than in the elementary school.

The students learn grammar, which gives the inner structure to language; we also must structure what we bring to expression in eurythmy. Verbs give motion to a poem, while nouns shape and hold the form together; an abstract noun holds differently from a concrete one, an active verb moves differently from a passive verb. You move forward, you move backward, and with each move something new comes to expression. The various prepositions are brought out through the different ways of bending the body. Bending and stretching express different things. The body is being consciously used in all its facets.

During the four high school years, the teaching of English literature is thus enriched by eurythmy. The students can have a fuller experience of poems, of ballads and drama, when they can move them rhythmically. The same is the case with music or languages. In particular, history and art can be enlivened to a deeper understanding through these movements.

Eurythmy in high school was taught in connection with other subjects they learn—not, however, from a more elaborate eurythmy understanding, which is available only after the high school age, when again a different approach is being taken, when teachers and parents join in regular eurythmy sessions.

Eurythmy was not invented or thought out, but rather discovered. Rudolf Steiner, in his research into the nature of the human being, discovered these movements within man himself, movements that have been built into the human body by nature, and that have become organic forms in man.

There is movement in every organic form, in every living thing. Discover the movement and transform it into movement of the whole body and you can express and even be, for a moment, that particular thing.

Our speech is still alive. Be speech for a moment! There is a tremendous movement in human speech when you enter into it and listen with your whole body. But in our day we have lost the feeling for sounds and words. We have forgotten the connection with the days when each human sound had a full meaning and value, and when each word sounded out its own meaning. We don't notice it anymore, unless we make an effort to listen with that special intent.

Only great poets notice it and use it in their poetic works. Think of Hopkins's "Sweet locks, loose locks, love locks, gay gear, going gallant, girl grace," or Shelley's "Wild west wind, thou breath of autumn's Being." The sounding of the words, the sounds themselves, tell so much more than the actual meaning.

When a eurythmy teacher chooses a poem for his class, he will consider the sound qualities and the rhythms in the poem, and make sure that sounds and rhythm coincide with the content that is to be expressed in the poem. A good example here is Tennyson's "He clasps the crag with crooked hands." In eurythmy it is the word that has to be brought into movement. The whole word, in its formative and musical expression, has to be made visible in eurythmy. The consonants are connected with the forming forces in everything that grows, with what we can see and perceive with our eyes: "Wave, corner, fire." The vowels are more musical to the ear, expressing feelings and emotions: Oh . . . ah.

Every sound in human speech expresses a particular quality, and each quality has a definite movement, which can be formed in a precise and clear shape while at the same time the same movement—for example, the K movement can be represented in space in as many different ways as the written letter on the page:

$$K K K k K K K K$$

but never arbitrarily, always in accordance with inner realities.

Our speech is built on clear lawfulness. Eurythmy is built on these same clear and objective laws. And still we must keep in mind that eurythmy is first and foremost an art. Eurythmy is a performing art, and out of this new art of movement has grown the pedagogical exercises as well as the therapeutic help that can be given through curative eurythmy.

Eurythmy is for all ages, from three to ninety-one years old, for all occasions, and for all purposes: to keep you well, flexible, slim; for festive celebration with eurythmy performances; or for joining actively in a eurythmy circle just for the joy of moving together in a relaxed and rhythmic art form. In doing it oneself, one will, step by step, come to understand that eurythmy is much more than what has been possible to bring out here. One will realize that eurythmy helps strengthen the inner being of man in his relation to the outer world, and in relation to himself as he reveals his whole being in his speech. Human speech underlies the eurythmy movement—yes, it *is* the eurythmy movement.

Its breathing gives movement,
Its sounding of words gives form,
Its thought pictures give content.

The audible speech with its sounding words, as well as the sounding tones in song and music, is being silenced and transformed into visible movements. The movement that is invisible, but audible in the sounding word or song, is to be made visible in the movement of the whole body. Audible sounds transformed into visible movements, into visible speech and visible song: that *is* eurythmy.

SOME EURYTHMY FORMS

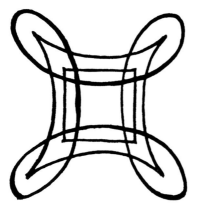

A. Harmonization of three different tempi

B. Rhythmic crescendo

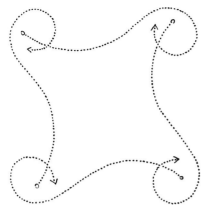

C. Rhythmic exercise developed by
Rudolf Steiner

D. Eurythmy exercise developed by
Rudolf Steiner

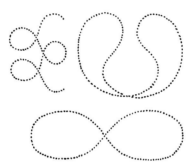

E. Metamorphosis of the figure eight

The need for imagination, a sense of truth and a feeling of responsibility—these are the three forces which are the very nerve of education.

— RUDOLF STEINER

HISTORY TEACHING—
A DRAMATIC ART

Henry Barnes

"Which of these Six Hundred individuals, in plain white cravat, that have come up to regenerate France, might one guess would become their king?"

Thus Thomas Carlyle, master of the dramatic historical moment, introduces his reader to Honoré Gabriel Riquetti de Mirabeau, destined to be the voice and soul of those men who came to Versailles in May 1789 to present their grievances and vote Louis XVI the money he so desperately needed, and who stayed to undo the regime that had summoned them and to lay the groundwork for the French Revolution.

Watercolor painting by a fifth grade student from the Greek Mythology main lesson

With broad, earthy brushstrokes Carlyle paints the portrait of that man "through whose shaggy beetle-brows, rough-hewn, seamed, carbuncled face, there look natural ugliness, small-pox, incontinence, bankruptcy—and burning fire of genius; like comet-fire glaring fuliginous through murkiest confusions . . . perhaps more French than any other man, and intrinsically such a mass of manhood too. Mark him well. The National Assembly were all different without that one; nay, he might say with the old Despot: the National Assembly! I am that!"

What would the history teacher do without Carlyle, Shakespeare, Schiller, Moliere, C. F. Meyer, Hermann Grimm, Albert Steffen, who as dramatists, biographers, essayists, poets, show him how to take the raw material of historical events and personalities and let them speak and act so that the character of an epoch, a moment of transition, a change in consciousness, a supersensible reality, reveal themselves through them in much the same way that a Rembrandt portrait reveals human character through the browns and golds and umbers of pigment on canvas? This is the art of symptomatology, the lifeblood of history and of history teaching.

History as we usually know it is largely a *fable convenue*. Trained by a material science that accepts as knowledge only that which can be observed with the physical senses or deduced from such observation—admitting as evidence only what can be weighed, counted, measured—the student of history has allowed himself to be persuaded that all history is the working of cause and effect in the physical realm. In the nineteenth century he was caught up by the seductive thought that history could indeed be an objective science from which all value judgments, all intuitive, subjective perceptions, would be sternly excluded. Karl Marx declared that man is an economic animal and that the ideals of art, culture, and religion are merely bourgeois ideological foam cast up by economic waves in the ocean of material reality. All history, therefore, in Marxist eyes, comes to be regarded as the history of class struggle, the survival of the fittest in human society.

But how are we to understand a Jeanne d'Arc, a Beethoven, a Giotto, a Giordano Bruno, a Buddha, a Christ? Were they merely the product of economic forces, of physical inheritance, and the impact of their environment? The student who approaches history with an open mind knows that there are impulses that strike through into evolution that cannot be explained as the effects of previous historical causes. They are original and decisive and, in some cases, introduce new stages of human experience. Such personalities, such events and achievements, become signposts pointing to the invisible field of formative forces working behind the scenes of outer history, shaping external circumstances into a language that can be read, just as one learns to read black marks on a white page

Mosaic by a sixth grade student for the Roman History main lesson

and enters, through them, into another world of thought and experience. It is for help in learning to read these symptoms and, as a teacher, in learning to shape them for the perceptive inner eye of his students, that the historian turns to the dramatist as a master of the art. But if it is to the dramatist that the history teacher looks for his art, it is to the spiritual scientist that he must look for insight into the underlying reality. And it is just at this point that the historian finds himself at the crossroad of his time—that crossroad to which, sooner or later, every one of us must come.

Here we all face the fundamental questions: Are there forms of knowledge not subject to tangible, material proof that are nevertheless valid? Are we forever shut off from knowledge of the spirit? Are we prepared to ask ourselves what makes a conclusion "scientific" and, therefore, valid? Is it the *content* or the *method* by which it is arrived at? If, as the spiritual science first put forward by Rudolf Steiner claims, it is now possible to extend the methods of disciplined, reproducible, fully conscious scientific inquiry to the realm of the supersensible, then the student of history may no longer arbitrarily dismiss the results of such investigation but must bring to them the same open-mindedness that he would wish to bring to any knowledge he encounters for the first time.

The historian who open-mindedly pursues this new path of knowledge comes to realize that history is not an endless repetition of the same, but that humanity in different epochs was different in fundamental ways. The Greek, for instance, experienced the world with a very different consciousness than the early Egyptian or Sumerian, or than the man of today. To learn to "read" these transformations in consciousness through the symptomatic historical details becomes the central task of the student of history. And the student who becomes a teacher of history has the further task to translate what he has "read" into the language of experience of his pupils. This is especially so for the class teacher in a Waldorf school, who accompanies the same group of children for a number of years and has, therefore, the privilege and the responsibility of leading his children up to the experience of their own time through the great stages of cultural evolution.

Having lived in the world of the fairy tale, legend, and myth in the first four grades, the children are ready in fifth grade, when they are ten, to enter that wonderful borderland between mythology and history proper. They have heard the stories of the Old Testament in third grade and have experienced in their powerful pictures the historical development of a unique people; and the following year, in the fourth grade, they have lived with dramatic intensity and delight in the stories of Norse mythology. Now in fifth, they begin where history emerges from the dawn of prehistory in that most ancient culture that arose under the guidance of initiate leaders in northern India. All that has come down to us in the form of the earliest sacred texts, the Hindu Vedas, are only the echoes of the original culture that lived as oral tradition long before a written language existed. Spiritual science, however, describes a culture of high spirituality that looked back with longing to a golden age—the Krita Yuga—when mankind felt itself united with its own world of divine origins. Through the ancient Hindu legends of creation, the stories of Manu, the great leader and teacher of his people; through the Mahabharata and the Ramayana, the epics of ancient Sanskrit literature, in the first of which the Bhagavadgita, the Celestial Song, is embedded, and even through the verses from the Rig-Veda itself, the children receive glimpses of civilization that resisted too deep an involvement with the world of the senses, the world of Maya, illusion, from which desires and entangling passions spring. The lofty ideal that Gautama Buddha taught thousands of years later, the ideal of freedom from the wheel of rebirth through the attainment of enlightenment and the entry into Nirvana, which is so fundamentally foreign to the Western soul, becomes understandable to a child's feeling through what he hears about the earliest origins of this first oriental culture.

Their history lessons then lead the children to experience how the impulse of civilization passes to a sister culture, the Avestan, in the high valleys of the plateau of Iran, in which man's interest turned from inner realities to the outer and now, once again under initiate leadership, he learns to cultivate the earth, to ennoble the wild grasses, and to domesticate the wild beasts. In the service of Ahura Mazdao, the spiritual sun, the ancient Iranian developed a settled agriculture and left behind his earlier nomadic existence. He experienced life as a duality, a struggle between the cosmic powers of light and darkness—Ahura Mazdao and Ahriman—and on earth between the progressive Iranian farmer and the Turanian nomad. Zarathustra, in the Zend Avesta, taught him to recognize and to serve Ahura Mazdao and, in doing so, to transform the earth and make it fruitful. Here the children experience a culture that finds its deepest fulfillment in service to the earth, but to a living earth still united with the spiritual cosmos.

Only at the beginning of the third epoch, at the time of the pyramid builders in Egypt and the Sumerians in the Tigris-Euphrates valleys, do the children find themselves for the first time in an age that has left us monuments, works of art, and written records on papyri and clay tablets. Here they are introduced to a culture no longer at one with the divine world from which it sprang. The active powers of the universe have partially withdrawn and left their handiwork as visible signs of their original creative presence. That divine creative powers had been at work, the ancient Babylonian or Egyptian felt strongly from the lawfulness and beauty of the world he came to know, and he became the great recorder of this cosmic harmony. He developed number systems with which to express time and space; he constructed temples and pyramids into which he built cosmic measures and relationships; he covered the walls of his tombs and temples with the records of

Watercolor painting by a sixth grade student from the Roman History main lesson

heavenly wisdom. Life was a preparation for death; one passed from the temporary "inn" of physical existence to meet Osiris in the West. *The Book of the Dead*, for the Egyptian, meant the *Chapters of the Coming Forth by Day*. Geometry and even agriculture had their inspiration in the temples. They were divine sciences, and man had to become a pupil in the mysteries to learn to unlock their secrets. The universe was still a divine creation and the earth was to be worked with according to cosmic laws, but the direct experience of divine being was fading and only its outer manifestations remained.

With the transition to Greece the children feel they have "come home," they are themselves young "Greeks" at this moment in their own development. Never before and never again will they enjoy this same beautiful harmony and balance. No longer do they trip along on tiptoe with the "heavenly" lightness of a very small child, nor have they yet succumbed to gravity and the weight of their maturing, earthly bodies. They move joyfully, with freedom and grace: heaviness and lightness, earth and heaven are, for this fleeting moment, in friendly balance and, within their souls, the living, fluid power of the imagination has not yet yielded to the self-conscious, critical intelligence and they are blessed with a natural harmony of soul experience in which the awakening faculty of analytic, conceptual thought is still carried within the protective sheath of a dreamlike feeling in the healthy, undamaged child. All this calls forth a special resonance in a child who is introduced to Greek civilization just at this time in his development. No longer do heavens overshadow the earth in Greek experience; man has become a joyful citizen of this world but he is not yet sunk and lost in its materialism. The physical is permeated by the ideal; Greek sculpture lives and is ideally human; the temples are in human balance and can therefore be the homes of the gods. Rhythm is everywhere, penetrates everything. The world beyond the senses, beyond death, is growing dim. The physical world is lighting up. For the Greek it was "better to be a beggar in the land of the living than a king in the realm of the shades." The Greek is wrestling with the problem of death; in its modern meaning, death was a new experience for mankind, and in man's inner world the earlier picture wisdom was yielding to the new consciousness of conceptual thought. Plato, the pupil of Egypt, still thought in cosmic images. His pupil Aristotle laid the foundations for the logical, rational world to come. And his pupil Alexander carried Hellenistic thought to every corner of the ancient world.

In the sixth grade, history study leads to Rome and the Middle Ages. Gone is the classic harmony of Greece, and the final descent into the material world has begun. Law, government, empire receive the stamp of personality. The sculptured Greek ideal of human beauty becomes the Roman portrait bust. The Greek *polis*, with its community of free, male citizens—a limited but very human social organism—gives way to the republic and then the empire of Rome. The Caesars violate the mysteries, forcing their initiation for purposes of personal power, and Rome becomes a kind of marketplace of world religions. Mystery wisdom, which still irradiated Greek culture, loses its reality and depth and is driven to the surface of life as an eclectic, and frequently debased, melting pot of philosophical schools and outer religious forms. And it is into this time of radical transition that Christ was born, that he lives, dies, and is resurrected. What had been experienced within the ancient mysteries as the death and resurrection of the soul becomes physical reality. The being that had been sought and worshiped in the cosmic sun enters earth existence, dwelling for three years in the body of Jesus of Nazareth, and unites, through death and resurrection, with the earth and the stream of human evolution. Within the downfall of the outer forms of civilization that have come down from the past and have gradually lost their connection with the world of their original divine creation, the seed of new beginning is implanted. Life and death, and with them human history, receive a new meaning.

The history curriculum leads on through the fall of Rome and the barbarian migrations into the so-called Dark Ages, with the impact of Islam and the emergence of a more or less stable feudal society in medieval times. The fourth cultural epoch draws to a close. The Greco-Roman ideal has flowed into that of a universal Christendom, administered by the all-encompassing Church, which speaks with the authority of Christ Jesus himself through his earthly vicar, the bishop of Rome. Latin is the language of the sacraments and of the scholarly world, and the Church, exercising authority in the temporal realm through the emperor and the feudal hierarchy, penetrates every aspect of medieval society, regulating, rewarding, punishing, administering justice, granting asylum, educating, building, fostering the arts, and influencing trade, commerce, and the entire feudal community in countless ways. The living culture of Greece and the form of Rome, infused with an outer Christianity, have merged in an all-pervasive European tradition that works as suggestive power into the feelings of medieval men and women. The individual still felt himself a member of a social community that had its authority in some dim and distant divine revelation that had come down as custom and tradition from the past. He was embedded instinctively in a social organism that supported and sustained him no matter how difficult his individual destiny might be.

But out of the depths of the evolutionary process, working through individuals and through events, a new impulse stirs and struggles for expression. Many times what was trying to break through took destructive and abortive forms, but there could be no doubt that something new was striving to awaken.

In the early fourteenth century, for instance, the universal hegemony of the Roman Church was suddenly challenged when a rising national power, France, under Philip the Fair, dared lay hands on the Pope and, in 1309, set up a rival Papacy in Avignon. The indivisible body of a united Christendom had two heads and was rent by a moral schism.

In 1411 Jan Hus publishes his call for a return of the Church to the original teachings of Christ and in 1415 is burned at the stake by order of the Council of Constance. An individual raises his voice to challenge the authority of the all-ruling Church.

An unlettered maid comes out of Lorraine and, at the behest of angelic voices, leads the feeble prince of France to his coronation in Rheins (1429), turning the tide in driving the English out of France, thus essentially resolving the Hundred Years' War and bringing about the separation of England and France, which freed each people to pursue its own national destiny in the modern world.

Charcoal drawing by an eighth grade student

In 1415 the Portuguese capture the Moorish citadel of Ceuta in North Africa, and in 1440 a prince of Portugal who was also Grand Commander of the Order of Christ establishes a school and research institute to gather all that can be known and observed pertaining to investigation, ship design, mapmaking, and geography as his ships push slowly southward along the coast of Africa. Henry the Navigator fought at Ceuta, starting out as a last, late medieval crusader but lived to spend his mature years as one of the first great champions of objective knowledge derived from direct observation of the physical environment. The school at Sagres laid the foundation for the mighty tide of exploration that swept the Portuguese around Africa and Columbus and many others to the New World, and culminated in Magellan's great voyage of circumnavigation in the sixteenth century.

Nowhere do the symptoms speak more clearly of the transition to a new consciousness than in the emerging world picture that gradually replaced the earth-centered view of the Middle Ages based on Ptolemy and the Greek tradition. The class teacher dealing with history in the seventh grade has the task to find those symptomatic details that best express the revolution in man's view of himself and of the world that characterized the fifteenth, sixteenth, and seventeenth centuries, the age of the Renaissance, of the Reformation, and of Exploration and Discovery. By way of illustration, let us look briefly at a sequence of personalities who were instrumental in establishing the modern world conception.

Nicolaus Copernicus (1473–1543), painter, physician, doctor of canon law, administrator, governor, mathematician, astronomer, inventor, political scientist—true man of the Renaissance yet devoted son and servant of the Church. The story is told of him that while studying in Italy, he was traveling on a boat in the quiet waters of the Adriatic and noticed what countless others before him had observed, that the shore appeared to be moving while he seemed to be standing still. Unlike the many others who had experienced the same illusion, it was in Copernicus's soul that the thought struck: could it be that it is the ship of the earth that turns in the heavens, and the sun and the fixed stars that appear to move but actually stand still? In Copernicus, a human soul is ready to resist the overwhelming authority of sense perception and transition that tell him that the sun rises and sets, that the stars rise, wheel across the sky, and descend in the west, and to set against this authority the assertion of his individual power of mind that can challenge the accepted view and think a thought that is in opposition to what mankind has seen, and been told, since the beginning of time. Copernicus returns to Poland and devotes the remaining thirty-eight years of his life to his duties to the Church and to observation of and thought about the stars. For twenty-seven years he works on his great book, *De Revolutionibus Orbium Coelestium*, rewriting its five thousand pages three times by hand,

and daring only to send it by trusted messenger to Nürnberg to be printed at the close of his life. Daring as Copernicus's conceptions were, he was still so much a man of the Middle Ages that he could not conceive that the planets might move in other orbits than concentric circles around the sun, because the circle is the most perfect of all forms. The deep devotion of a pious soul united with the observation of a great natural philosopher came to expression in such remarks as: "To look up at the sky and behold the wondrous works of God must make a man bow his head and heart in silence. . . . All I can do is to adore when I behold this unfailing regularity, this miraculous balance and perfect adaptation. The majesty of it all humbles me to the dust."

Copernicus is followed by Tycho Brahe (1546–1601), Danish noble, cantankerous personality, and supreme observer of the heavens, whose painstaking accuracy so impressed his brilliant younger colleague, Johannes Kepler (1571–1630), that he threw out two years' work on the orbit of Mars because he could not reconcile his calculations with Brahe's observations, although he came within eight-tenths of a degree of doing so. It was only by starting over that Kepler came to the amazing conclusion that Mars moves in an elliptical orbit around the sun with the sun in one of its two foci:

> Since the divine goodness has given us in Tycho Brahe a most careful observer, from whose observations the error of 8' is shown in this calculation . . . it is right that we should with gratitude recognize and make use of this gift of God. . . . As they could not be neglected, these 8' alone have led the way towards the complete reformation of astronomy.

Thus destiny united the eagle-eyed observer, who could not fully penetrate the observations with mathematical thought, and the younger genius, whose mathematical intelligence could penetrate the mass of observed data and make it yield up its hidden laws, but whose physical eyes were weak and useless for observing the actual stars. For less than two years they worked together in Castle Benatchek near Prague, and from their collaboration came the three fundamental laws on which all modern astronomy is based.

Five years after the death of Copernicus a boy is born in southern Italy, near Naples, who finally fled the Church for which he was destined and became a wandering scholar and teacher of the new doctrines. Only his daring mind left nothing fixed, not even the universe itself. The story is told of Giordano Bruno that, as a boy, having looked out across the valley from his native Mt. Cicale toward Vesuvius, he observed that the slopes of the distant mountain appeared blue and barren, whereas he knew his own environs as vine-covered and fertile. One day he hiked across the valley to Vesuvius and saw that it was as verdant as his own slopes, and when he looked back across the valley to Mt. Cicale,

Ninth grade chalk drawing for the History through Art main lesson

to his astonishment it appeared as barren and blue as Vesuvius had once seemed. Out of this experience, so the story goes, the idea entered his mind and took hold of his soul that one's view of the world depends on where one stands, that knowledge is not absolute but relative. Bruno went on to teach that space is infinite, that the fixed stars are themselves suns, and that the sun with all its planets is in motion.

> There are innumerable worlds like ours, throned and sphered amidst the ether . . . of these stars alone none is in the middle but the universe is immeasurable in all its parts. . . . For the center of the universe is neither the sun nor in the sun, neither the earth nor in the earth, nor in any place whatsoever. They are free in space, attracting each other, and moving by their own inward spiritual power.

Ink drawing by a seventh grade student

Poet, musician, humanist scholar, Bruno had a fiery spirit and it was by fire that he died on February 17, 1600, in Rome, condemned to death by the Church because he refused to abandon the truth as he knew it. "It may be you fear more to deliver judgment upon me than I fear judgment," he said to those who condemned him. "For I esteem all fame and all victory displeasing to God, and most vile and worthless if there is not truth in them; and for the love of true wisdom and learning I am full of weariness; I am crucified and tormented." "Touch me, O God," he had written in a sonnet, "and I shall be as it were a flame of fire."

Thirty-three years later, in the same church in Rome, Santa Maria Sopra Minerva, another man knelt before an Inquisition court and was forced to recant his heretical views. Seventy years of age, he was famous for having brought the moon, the planets, even the sun itself into man's earthly vision by means of his new telescope. The moon, he had demonstrated, shone only by reflected light and had a face rugged and cratered like some desolate earthly desert, and it was he, Galileo Galilei, who had observed that the radiant divinity of the sun itself was marked by shadows that came and went. He had wrested the laws of falling bodies, of the swinging pendulum, of the path of projectiles, of the refracting lens, from the information conveyed to him by his sense; he had laid the foundations for physical science and technology for the coming centuries; and, perhaps, more important even, he had lent his authority to the principle that only that which can be expressed in the objective language of mathematics can be accepted as valid knowledge. The primary qualities in all phenomena are those that can be counted, weighed, and measured; all others—sensations, thoughts, feelings, moral judgments—are subjective and therefore secondary in ascertaining the truth. "He who would solve scientific questions without the aid of mathematics, undertakes the impossible. One must measure what is measurable, and make measurable what is not already."

Condemned to house arrest, Galileo lived for another nine years and completed his second principal written work, the *Discorsi*, on the laws of motion. He was ill, lonely, and growing rapidly blind. In 1638 he wrote:

Ah! Your poor friend and servant is entirely and incurably blind. This heaven, this earth, this universe, that I have extended a thousand times beyond the limits of the past epochs by wonderful observation, have now shrunk to the narrow confines of my own body. Thus God likes it; so, I too, must like it!

He died on January 8, 1642.

It was on Christmas Day of that same year (Old Style) that a baby was born prematurely in Woolsthorpe, England, who was so sickly and tiny at birth that his mother said a quart pot would easily have held him. He grew up with extraordinary powers of concentration, and, entering Cambridge University with little more than a knowledge of elementary arithmetic, he nevertheless achieved his discoveries of differential calculus, the composition of light, and gravitational theory before he was twenty-six. Deeply immersed in mystical pursuits, he seemed to resent his mathematical genius. Once he understood something, he appeared to lose interest in it. At forty-two, after publishing his masterwork, the *Principia*, Isaac Newton abandoned mathematics and science for the rest of his life. Toward the end of his life, Newton wrote:

> I do not know what I may appear to the world; but to myself I seem to have been only like a boy playing on the sea-shore and diverting myself in now and then finding a smoother pebble or a prettier shell than ordinary, whilst the great ocean of Truth lay all undiscovered before me.

At his death in 1727 he was accorded a splendid funeral and buried in Westminster Abbey, a fact that deeply impressed Voltaire, who was in England at the time.

Thus we have in Isaac Newton the intellectual genius who could translate the intuitive thoughts of a Giordano Bruno into mathematical formulas and reduce the "miraculous balance" still experienced by a Copernicus to an equation expressing the power of gravitational force on any solid body in physical space. The mathematical basis for a mechanical universe had been achieved, and by a mind almost indifferent to its achievement. Within a period of two hundred years the human soul had abandoned its naively realistic but essentially spiritual worldview and had constructed a mechanical model according to mathematical principles in its stead. Mankind's loss was the loss of the last vestiges of an imaginative world conception, but for this it had gained a new capacity—objective, disciplined, intellectual thought. At an elementary, still-childlike level, this is the experience of the seventh grade. With this behind us we enter the final year of grammar school and find ourselves on the doorstep of the present day.

Eighth- and ninth-graders, young people of thirteen to fourteen and fourteen to fifteen years, are hungry for the experience of their own time. The eighth-grader is at the end of the period of pictorial, imaginative perception and still relishes biographical narrative and dramatic events. Dawning in the ninth-grader is the ability to grasp ideas, to generalize, and to perceive a lawful principle at work in a panorama of personalities and events. The history curriculum in both eighth and ninth grades recommends dealing with modern history, essentially from the late seventeenth century to the present day. In the younger class it will, hopefully, still be the class teacher who teaches the history, and in the ninth the children will, for the first time, meet a specialist in this subject area. Class teacher and specialist should consult together, which by no means implies that they should avoid all repetition of subject matter, as it can be most beneficial to cover the same ground from a new and different point of view.

A very real responsibility rests on the shoulders of the history teacher in these years. The symptomatic events that crowd the stage in the nineteenth and twentieth centuries speak of the destruction of the old, and there are relatively very few that point to the birth of what is new. What began in the fourteenth and fifteenth and went on into the sixteenth seventeenth, and eighteenth centuries, engendering so much enthusiasm, hope, and often heroic sacrifice—the assertion of individuality, the exploration of the physical world, the evolution of parliamentary democracy, the rise of liberal, scientific thought, the emergence of modern nation states—moved inexorably toward a high tide of materialism, toward industrialization and technology; exploration of the natural and human environment; political, economic, and social polarizations; totalitarianism; and ruthless war. Although the fourteen- to fifteen-year-old is fascinated by the World Wars, the rise of Hitler, the emergence of Communism, the East-West conflict, he is at a very tender moment in his development. His newly emancipating gift of intellectual thought seeks ideals to give it direction, confidence, and inner support, without which he is easily a prey to confusion, self-doubt, emotional pressures, and an eroding discouragement, against which he has not yet the maturity to protect himself. The history teacher, therefore, faces a real dilemma and a challenging pedagogical task. Where, indeed, is he to turn for help in an age that characteristically gives rise to insoluble problems in almost every sphere of life?

The teacher of history has returned to the original crossroad from which he once set out as a student. Having once chosen the road leading toward spiritual science and what it has to say about the historical past, he must renew this direction and once again call on spiritual science to shed its light on the dark and confusing picture that our time presents to external view. Let us follow one central thread in the tangled skein of modern history as spiritual science illuminates it for us as an example of the search for the new and positive in the midst of the disintegration of the old.

The late eighteenth and early nineteenth centuries brought to birth an extraordinary configuration of personalities—artists, poets, philosophers, naturalists—whom we know as members of the Romantic Movement, as the German Idealists, as Transcendentalists in America. In Middle Europe they included some of the greatest artists and spiritual thinkers of their time: Goethe, Schiller, Novalis, Herder, Schelling, Fichte, and many more. In England we think of Wordsworth, Shelley, Keats, Coleridge, and in our own

Chalk drawing by an eighth grade student for the American History main lesson

country, some years later, Emerson, Thoreau, Hawthorne, Melville. These were cosmopolitan spirits, who looked across national boundaries to their fellow writers and thinkers, feeling themselves to be, first of all, citizens of a spiritual republic and only secondly members of a given people or nation. The Middle Europeans in particular, living as they did in the many small kingdoms and principalities that at that time constituted "Germany," regarded themselves as representatives of culture rather than political personalities; they thought in European and human terms, seeking to bridge East and West and build a "middle ground."

And it was at this time that the revolution erupted in France, casting up the three ideals of liberty, equality, fraternity that flashed for a brief, chaotic moment against the horizon of the times. In the form in which they then arose they were mutually contradictory: equality was incompatible with liberty, and fraternity, very often, with both; but one could sense behind them a powerful undercurrent of social yearning, desperately seeking a harmonious, organic form. Goethe, apparently uninterested in the revolution,

nevertheless declared while observing the battle of Valmy in 1872, "From this spot and from this moment a new epoch of world history begins." At another level, however, he gave poetic expression to the impulse stirring beneath the surface of his time in his mysterious fairy tale *The Green Snake and the Beautiful Lily*, translated into English by Thomas Carlyle. Told by one of the German émigrés who had been forced by the French armies to flee from their homes west of the Rhine, the fairy tale embodies in picture form the germinal idea of a new social order in which the three forces in human social life find their harmonious balance within the whole.

In 1806 Napoleon dissolved the remnants of the Holy Roman Empire of the German Nation and consolidated numerous German territories into the Confederation of the Rhine, thereby planting the germ of political centralization and an independent national state into the minds and hearts of the German people. A second generation of idealists arose now, imbued with a political liberalism and fired with a dawning nationalism that first awoke in opposition to Napoleon. Their hopes and dreams climaxed in the revolutions of 1848 and were finally talked to death in the Parliament in Frankfort, before these idealists offered an unacceptable crown to Frederick William IV of Prussia and all hopes collapsed completely.

With contempt for the liberal, democratic, would-be revolutionaries, Otto von Bismarck saw that Germany would only be united by "blood and iron," which, becoming Prussian chancellor in 1862, he straight away proceeded to do. In January 1871, in Louis XIV's Hall of Mirrors in Versailles, Bismarck proclaimed Wilhelm I Kaiser of the Second German Empire, and the stage was set for World War I. The European ideal carried by a cosmopolitan, Christian impulse that might have served as a balancing force in world affairs was effectively suppressed and submerged by a materialistic, economic, political, and military power that challenged the existing order and inevitably led Germany into the destructive two-front war that Bismarck's diplomacy had sought by all means to avoid. The war ended in a so-called peace that led, in its turn, to World War II.

And it was the First World War that more than any other event set its stamp on the outer history of our time, and within the catastrophe of the four and a half years of war it was perhaps the year 1917 above all that proved to be the historical watershed of the twentieth century, forever separating the world of the eighteenth and nineteenth centuries from the world that was to come. In April 1917 Woodrow Wilson led this country, to which he had promised peace in 1916, into the war, and in the same month the German high command sent a sealed train through their own lines from Switzerland to inject

Watercolor painting by a fifth grade student for the Egyptian History main lesson

the bacillus into the sick body of Russia that, they hoped, might bring about its final collapse and swiftly end the war in the east, freeing the German armies to turn their full remaining strength against France and Britain in the west. Lenin proved a more powerful agent than anyone could have dreamed, due in great part to the fact, as Rudolf Steiner pointed out at the time, that the liberal democratic government that had come to power when the czar abdicated in March had no original creative ideas capable of effecting the moral leadership Russia needed. Instead, a vacuum was created into which was swept, as if by suction, the ruthless organizing genius of Lenin, with a microscopic but absolutely disciplined revolutionary minority at his command.

Thus, within a month, the two powers who were destined to struggle for world domination found themselves in motion toward their unknown goals. America, led by a professor and abstract theorist, remote from practical reality, steps out for the first time on the world's political stage. Russia, infected by materialistic, Marxist dogma, plunges from a semifeudal, agrarian, mystically religious state into the industrialized twentieth century, and, in 1918–1919, the two youthful, awakening, political and economic giants confront each other for the first time across the exhausted, wounded body of Western and Central Europe.

But, unnoticed, there was also a third force at work at this time. Men and women from the seventeen nations within sound of guns along the Rhine were working together in the northwest of neutral Switzerland to build a structure of carved wood that was to be a house for the living Word, a Goetheanum, built in continuation of the impulse that had once inspired the artists and thinkers of the late eighteenth and early nineteenth centuries. The building's architect had united in his design, and in his life's work as well, the two realms symbolically represented in Goethe's fairy tale as the realm of the Green Snake and that of the Beautiful Lily. Physical and spiritual reality were interwoven in an organic, harmonious whole.

The key to his achievement lay in an idea that had ripened within him through three decades and, in 1917, found its first comprehensive statement in a little-known work published under the title *The Riddles of the Soul.* In this work Rudolf Steiner points out that man is a threefold being and that his soul faculties of thinking, feeling, and will are reflected in three autonomous but closely and harmoniously interacting organic systems: the nervous and sense organization; the rhythmic, circulatory system of lungs and heart; and the metabolic organism together with the limbs. He shows how each has its own form and functions and serves as the organic instrument for the three activities of the soul. From this starting point, Steiner went on to show that the social organism likewise can be seen to comprise three interacting but nevertheless independent spheres of social action: the economic realm, in which necessity holds sway; the cultural-spiritual sphere, in which each person participates as a free individual according to his or her individual gifts; and the sphere of justice and of political rights, in which all are, or should be, equal, thanks to the simple fact that each is human. If each aspect of the social organism were allowed to develop according to its innate character and needs, the ideal of brotherhood would make itself felt in the economic sphere, religion, and the arts; and a much reduced political organization would be responsible to see that a fair balance is maintained between the rights of the individual and the larger community. Seen in this light, the ideals of the French Revolution become mutually compatible and each works together for the good of the whole. The impulse that struggled chaotically for realization in the 1790s and that lived as an ideal in the minds and hearts of the cosmopolitan spirits of that time finds a new birth in our time—in the midst of the very polarities that threaten to destroy the world. For an eighth-grader this remains a picture; for the ninth-grader it can become a dawning conception; for a twelfth-grader it can be a confirmation of the meaning of history as he or she has come to know it during the course of his or her schooling, and can become the basis for renewed confidence in life.

In an article such as this there can be no thought of presenting Rudolf Steiner's social philosophy or the ideas of underlying Waldorf education with anything even approaching completeness; they can serve only to illustrate how the insights of spiritual science can become fruitful in a particular field—in teaching of history. Young people seek meaning; without thinking or speaking about it, they want to be reassured that this is the life they were meant to lead. A teaching of history that becomes a true symptomatology, through which the realities underlying human evolution speak a clear and convincing language, can be an important factor, no matter how unconsciously, in confirming the resolution to be born on earth at this time.

HIGH SCHOOL PHYSICS AND CHEMISTRY

Hans Gebert

Social conditions are changing so rapidly that high school graduates are best prepared for life if they are able and willing to continue learning and to change their occupations in response to social need. A flexible and acute mind, an open heart for the conditions of others, a fine sensibility for the true and beautiful, and knowledge of the complexities of modern life are some of the most desirable results of education.

This is why subjects are taught not only for their intrinsic value but for their ability to:

1. develop such personal faculties as clear thinking, sensitive feelings, and strong will;
2. establish relations between students and their natural and social environment;
3. evoke appreciation for the complex currents and forces shaping our lives today.

Using two examples based on classroom experience, I want to show how physics and chemistry can be used as what might be called educational tools to accomplish these purposes. Different subject matter could be used for the same ends; in fact, it is improbable that a visitor to several schools would find exactly the same subject matter used in any two of them.

A Ninth-Grade Physics Module

The work centers around the automobile. Part of each lesson is devoted to learning how the main systems of the motorcar work. Starting with the engine, students learn in detail the cycle of operation in each cylinder: drawing in the mixture of vaporized gas and air, compressing and thereby heating it, causing it to explode by passing a spark through it, pushing out the combustion products. The valves in the engine and the distributor in the electrical system have to be synchronized so that the spark comes just at the right moment and the burned gases are eliminated in time for the intake of the next portion of mixture. Gradually it becomes clear how this is done, and how the engine, once started, recharges the battery for the next start, and how it generates the voltage for producing sparks.

Next the class learns how the power of the engine is transmitted to the wheels. When starting, a great deal of force is necessary to get the car much moving; when we are cruising on a level road, the driving force can be much less—it need only overcome road and air resistance. The students learn about the clever ways engineers have found of changing the driving force as required by driving conditions. Work like this makes demands on the intellectual understanding of the students. As they will be expected to make accurate drawings and to write lucid descriptions of the processes, their skill in drawing and writing and their thinking powers develop. At the same time, they experience how human ingenuity is able to arrange valves, cogs, and belts in such an ingenious way that an essentially destructive force, like the explosion of a gas-air mixture, is put to good use. To make the point vividly, the teacher might describe disasters caused by the explosion of similar mixtures accidentally ignited by sparks.

Understanding how such potentially explosive forces are controlled is especially relevant for students in the ninth grade. They are just at the height of puberty, experiencing new and potentially explosive forces arising in their own organism. They experience, too, that these inner forces often get them into trouble, much of which could often be avoided by a little thought. However, the right thoughts have an annoying habit of coming at the wrong time, and thinking does not yet seem to be quite strong enough to help in coping with the explosive puberty forces. The study of the automobile, showing as it does a result of the conquest of the heat forces in nature by the human intellect, gives courage to the students in their developmental predicament. The choice of this subject matter at the ninth-grade stage is an example of how the Waldorf teacher tries to further the development of the student by choice of subject matter.

While the working of the automobile is dealt with in one part of the lesson every day, the history of the heat engines can be treated in another part of the lesson. The first heat engines were very crude pumping engines used in mines in England. The first major improvements were made by James Watt. These improvements were so important that many people are under the impression that Watt actually invented the steam engine. As a young man, Watt worked as a laboratory technician at the University of Glasgow, Scotland. The theoretical work on heat that Professor Joseph Black was carrying out at the university when Watt was there could well have inspired some of Watt's ideas for improving the heat pump. While dealing with this section of history we have an opportunity to

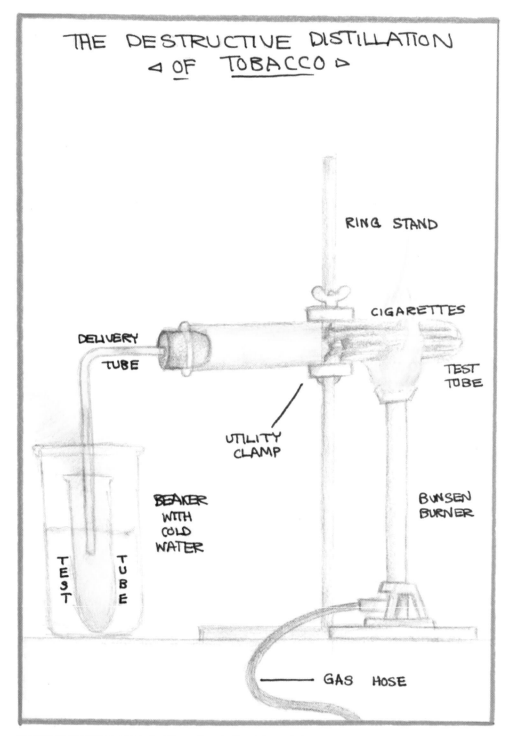

Drawing by an eighth grade student for an Organic Chemistry main lesson

teach the fundamental laws of science discovered by Black. At the same time, we are showing an example of the interaction of pure science and technology.

Later in Watt's career his engines were manufactured by the firm of Boulton and Watt in Birmingham, England, and they were leased, not sold, to mine owners. The legal arrangements associated with these leases made it necessary to measure the work done by engines when using a certain amount of coal. This is a good starting point for talking about important concepts like energy, power, efficiency, and their measurement.

Both here and when describing Black's work, there is an opportunity for the students themselves to do some of the experiments connected with the measurement of heat and work. In this way they experience how scientific work is actually carried out. Before leaving high school they should have had this experience a few times—not to train them in experimental techniques but to let them take part in an activity that is important to our civilization.

The relation between Watt and his customers shows also how invention and science influence social conditions. The owners and managers were pleased that the new engines saved a lot of fuel in the mines. Soon, however, they were trying to find ways to avoid paying royalties to Boulton and Watt, and this may have been one of the incentives for the invention of the high-pressure steam engine that was necessary before locomotives could be built.

The consequent evolution of railways is another important chapter in the history of technology. This is interesting from a technological point of view but even more so as an example of the way in which technological progress is often opposed by vested interest. In England the canal owners fought tooth and nail against the establishment of the railways. These battles were fought out on the floor of the Houses of Parliament, and we have an opportunity to describe the parliamentary system at work in relation to quite a realistic problem. I have sometimes staged with classes the parliamentary debate about the licensing of the first proper railway in England from Manchester to Liverpool, giving the students a chance to deal with arguments for and against the establishment of railways.

We can also introduce two interesting and contrasting biographies. If any one man can be said to have invented the high-pressure steam engine, the man was Richard Trevithick. He was a prolific inventor and adapted the high-pressure steam engine to many uses, such as the propulsion of boats and ploughs. He also attempted to drill the first tunnel under the river Thames in London. He established pumping engines in the silver mines of Central America and lost all he had gained in that venture, when Bolivar drove out the Spaniards. In fact, all his projects were like the Thames tunnel: daring, imaginative, and ultimately unsuccessful; he died in poverty and hardly anyone knows of him nowadays.

George Stevenson's name is more familiar, but the widely held belief that he invented the locomotive is as unfounded as the belief that Watt invented the steam engine. Stevenson came from a very poor family in Yorkshire. With tenacity and perseverance he got an education for himself and for his son Robert. Together they built one locomotive after another until they had the best engine that could be constructed at that time. Stevenson devoted all his energies to locomotives and to the many details needed to organize a railway system. He became famous and died a rich man. These two biographies, simply told, convey more profound lessons to the students than any amount of theorizing and moralizing.

I hope the rather detailed description of the various aspects that would together constitute a physics module in the ninth grade has shown how the developmental stage of the student is considered, how faculties are trained appropriate to that stage, how psychological confidence is created at the same time that knowledge is imparted, and how the pupils experience the interaction of science, technology, and social conditions.

Chemistry—Ninth Through Eleventh Grades

In this example we shall be more concerned with the development of subject matter and how this can be adapted to the intellectual development of the pupils. At the same time I hope to show how the students can be given an experience of their relation to nature on the one hand and of the way in which the thinking about nature changed gradually and is still changing. This can be done implicitly without theorizing about philosophy, leaving the students to formulate their own questions and conclusions. As described for the physics module, the teaching would at each stage include historical, experimental, and biographical aspects of the subject.

The sequence starts in the ninth grade with a discussion of photosynthesis. This is the basic chemical reaction for life on earth; the plant manufactures sugars from the carbon dioxide of the air and the water taken up from the ground. Energy is supplied by light captured and suitably transformed by the green pigment chlorophyll; oxygen is released into the atmosphere. In grade school students will already have learned that oxygen is necessary for and is used up in burning and respiration, and photosynthesis appears now as the reaction that replaces the oxygen again.

The observable properties of sugars and the starch and cellulose developed from them are then discussed (not their formulas or structure—the concept of an element is introduced later). The characteristic smell of burning sugar and the stages of its combustion are observed, the beautiful color obtained when testing for the presence of sugar in a solution is shown, and the way in which sugar can liberate metals from their compounds and form metal mirrors is demonstrated; then we discuss the conversion of the other carbohydrates, cellulose and starch, into sugar. All this work is based on telling demonstration experiments in which powers of observation are trained and wonder is engendered.

Next the students meet fats and proteins, the other constituents of our food, and are shown where they arise in the organism of the plants. This leads on to a discussion of digestion, which will probably be a review of grade school work but which is now done in more detail and with more experiments. Other reactions will be discussed, such as the formation of alcohol and vinegar and the formation of esters and ethers. Industrial processes are also introduced, such as the manufacture of soap, paper, and plastics, the dry distillation of wood and coal, and the use of coal tar and petroleum in the manufacture of many objects in daily use. Time will, of course, permit a few such processes to be treated. The students get to know many different types of organic compounds, such as amino and fatty acids, alcohols, esters, eshers, aldehydes, and ketones—all in relation to biological or industrial processes.

Science teachers may object to this work on the grounds that there is no proper chemistry in it if they are accustomed to start chemistry by discussing the difference between compounds and elements or between physical and chemical change. To this a Waldorf teacher would reply that, on the contrary, a great deal of very meaningful chemistry is indeed taught. We are dealing with chemical reactions basic to everything that happens on earth. We begin the study at the very stage where it began on the earth. We begin the study at the very stage where it began historically: namely, with observable processes and their classification into different types. In addition, we meet the needs and interest of the students at this age by emphasizing how things happen. Only later does the why interest them. Up to the ninth grade and the beginning of the tenth grade it is, therefore, good to use their interest in the how to learn a large body of facts. These can then later be used as examples when the more basic, theoretical principles are developed.

In tenth grade the transition takes place from the how to the why phase. It is good at this stage to systematize what has been learned in the grade school about acids, bases, and salts, and oxidation and reduction. From there the transition can easily be made to the idea of a chemical element in relation to the chemical processes with which we start. We find base-forming and acid-forming elements, we find metals and nonmetals, we meet elements that are easily oxidized and others that resist oxidation. We can now show how surprisingly few elements enter into the reactions described in the ninth grade, and we can relate the properties of carbohydrates, fats, and proteins to the proportion of these few elements in the compounds.

As an example of the way in which the properties of an element are related to the chemical processes in mineral, plant, and animal, we can choose nitrogen. It is interesting to see how nitrogen can form bases and acids. Ammonium nitrate, for instance, is a salt whose basic and acidic parts are both derived from nitrogen. Nitrogen is also characteristic of protein. The name of the breakdown products of protein, "amino acids," reminds us of ammonia, a strong base, so "amino acid" is almost equivalent to "base-acid," a contradiction in terms! However, the life of man and animal is largely determined by polarities like pleasure-pain and courage-fear, polarities of soul experience that have to be able to swing from one extreme to the other rather easily. How interesting that the body of man and animal is also mainly made of protein with its nitrogen, swinging easily from base to acid and back! Plants do contain protein, of course, but only in small amounts. The main bulk of their bodies are made of carbohydrates containing no nitrogen. When we come to minerals constituting the stable crust of the earth, we must have salts with acidic and basic parts, each due to a different element. Or we have oxides of metals—calxes, as the alchemists would have called them—indicating by this word the loss of the shiny, sounding qualities of the metal through oxidation.

The tenth-grade chemistry module could culminate in a first, qualitative discussion of the periodic system of the elements.

When we get to the eleventh grade it is time to introduce the numerical laws of chemistry. We have now a great store of examples on which to draw—and can repeat suitable simple experiments quantitatively. Students will now be interested in a historical account of the way in which chemistry developed and in more philosophical questions. The history of the phlogiston theory of the eighteenth century and its gradual replacement by the oxygen theory of combustion shows scientists at work much in the same way in which they work today. The way in which the atomic theory was resuscitated by John Dalton at the beginning of the century, how it was accepted by some scientists and not by others, how there were periods in which the theory was rejected as fantastic and as too metaphysical by some of the most prominent chemists and physicists, make a fascinating story. The reasons given for rejection or acceptance are instructive, too. The module could culminate with a discussion of the discovery of radioactivity and the change in thinking it caused.

Such a treatment shows very well how scientific thought develops. It also raises profound questions about the nature of matter. The history can be continued in the physics and mathematics lessons and can show how the nature of space and time also came to be questioned. In fact, the students begin to experience the crisis in cognition of the turn of the century and are mature enough to face such fundamental questions. They also become aware how inadequate many apparently simple and neat solutions of problems can be.

I hope that these two examples show how physics and chemistry are used as "educational tools." Of course, they serve also as a foundation for future college courses. By no means do all students need such college preparatory courses, and in some Waldorf high schools additional science programs are run as electives for those who need them. However, the range of electives is always kept to the necessary minimum and every student has to take the core courses both in the sciences and in the humanities.

Naturally, the science lessons offer, above all, opportunities for developing logical, careful, and practical thinking. However, they also contribute to the development of a sense of responsibility toward our natural surroundings and toward society. They can awaken a feeling for the complex way in which scientific thought interacts with technology, philosophy, and social conditions. Teachers have the task of structuring the lessons so that science is taught truly humanely. They want to use the subject matter for developing human faculties at the right time. They want to convey some of the excitement that the human activity of scientific research affords its practitioners. They want to facilitate communication between the spheres of human endeavor and particularly between the sciences on the one hand and the arts on the other.

ABOUT CRAFTS

Margaret Frohlich

Teaching crafts in schools and camps generally means to "expose" the children to certain materials and tools and to let them "find out on their own" what they can do with them. The teacher is supposed to "interfere" as little as possible.

How does the teaching of crafts in a Waldorf school compare with this approach?

Like all other subjects, it is structured; the backbone of this structure is the child himself. We try to work with those elements that, at a given time, are foremost in the child's development.

The six-year-old is all rhythm: hopping, clapping, skipping. In teaching crafts we take advantage of this sense of rhythm: first-graders learn to knit. While the sense of rhythm is activated in the movement of the hands and fingers, concentration and coordination are also developed. These are two very important abilities, useful in all fields of life. And because one of our aims is the development of abilities, the actual process of *doing* is stressed rather than the finished product. For the same reason, boys and girls are learning the same things together. Why should only boys or only girls acquire a certain ability?

In every new project the children will be confronted with different problems. They will gradually learn to cope with the questions: What is it to be? How is it to be used? The answers will teach them how to plan their work: what materials to use, how to determine the shape of the project and its decoration. All craft projects are meant to be done for a useful rather than a merely decorative purpose.

Along with the dexterity of the fingers, the ability to plan one's work is very important. Later, when the children learn bookbinding, in the junior and senior years, they must already know how to plan. In bookbinding each step of the work is comparatively easy. Planning done in early years will be a solid foundation for work in the higher grades, and it certainly will help the children through life itself, in domestic, academic, and vocational activities.

This shows how important it is that each craft teacher know the whole curriculum from the first through the twelfth grade, even though he may only teach a limited number of

Scarf woven by a tenth grade student

grades. In teaching young children, he must know what foundation to lay in order to prepare them for what is to come. In the upper grades he ought to be able to anticipate certain skills and attitudes. But he must also know the curriculum of other subjects so that he can add to a theoretical subject the experience of the actual doing: in the sixth grade, for instance, the children are introduced to acoustics. They also learn about the historical development of the musical instrument. At the same time, they will learn in crafts how to make bamboo recorders, how to tune them, and how to play them.

Young children learn by imitation. In teaching the lower grades, the teacher will show the techniques to the children rather than explain the process intellectually. Explaining will be done in later years, when the children are more capable of grasping a thought.

Gradually new elements are brought in. In crocheting, which is begun in the second grade, there is still a strong element of rhythm involved. However, there are choices to be made. One can make a variety of different stitches: single or double crochet, chain stitch, and so on. One can go back and forth in parallel rows or in a circular movement around a center. Planning one's project is becoming more involved.

The first three grades are, in a way, a unit in which the basic processes of knitting and crocheting are taken up and gradually used on larger and more complicated projects, as, for instance, simple garments or toys. Just as one needs to learn the alphabet so that one can express oneself with written words, one also needs to learn the "alphabet" of the various crafts.

Yet there is much more to crafts than just certain techniques. We like to let the children work with natural fibers: wool, to begin with. Historically, knitting was first done by shepherds while they watched their flocks in the fields. With stories or poems about the little lamb, we try to stir the children's imagination. We also let them experience the material itself. How soft and light the wool fibers can be if twisted into a string! And out of such a string that used to be the little lamb's soft coat we are now making objects. For most first-graders this is an experience bordering on magic.

Whenever it is possible, we let them also see and experience sheep in nature. All this will help develop a feeling and respect for materials. After all, there is a great deal that nature and man have achieved in order to bring those materials about. It is important to be aware of this. Here the approach is the opposite of the one mentioned above, where children are "exposed" to materials and are encouraged to use them at will.

The attitude toward tools must also be considered: what are tools? Man has hands with which he can do certain things quite well. Yet he cannot fly like a bird, or swim like a fish, or run like a horse. But he can think. With his thinking he can build "extensions" to his hands with which he can outdo the one-sidedness of animals. These extensions are his helpers, his friends. Friends treated with care, understanding, and respect will help him master great difficulties. Negative results are also obvious in case he misuses them. This respectful attitude toward tools has nothing to do with their actual monetary value or their availability. One would not think of misusing one's hands, either.

This attitude toward materials and tools must be developed quite early in the children's school life and, hopefully, also at home.

Another attitude toward one's work also needs to be stressed right from the beginning. It is up to the teacher to suggest a project that lies within the scope of the child's abilities. But once the project has been started it must be carried through to the end. With everything we take on, we are shouldering a responsibility. And responsibilities must be taken seriously. Would a mother, while cooking a meal for the family, say, I do not feel like finishing it?

Teachers and parents often mistakenly think that standards in attitude or achievement ought to be low to begin with and then raised as the children grow older. But experience teaches us that this does not work. As a rule children are eager to do well and usually

Basket woven by a ninth grade student

Books made by eleventh and twelfth grade students

respond positively to a high standard provided they are given tasks that they can handle. They might groan momentarily, but in the long run they will be grateful and happy.

One hears so much about "self-expression" in the visual arts and in crafts. Expressing oneself is meant to be the goal of the activity. Aiming at self-expression is actually quite unnecessary, since all we do carries our personal stamp. That is what makes life so interesting and rich, that no two people do the same thing quite the same way. Just as our handwriting is entirely our own, even though we use the same letters of the alphabet, all other things we do will also bear our stamp.

When in the fourth and fifth grades the children learn to sew by hand and embroider, no two projects will look alike even though all children might have had the same task to do.

In the sixth grade stuffed animals and/or dolls are made. The children study geometry in the course of the sixth grade and hence are taught in crafts how to develop the pattern from their own design. It is interesting and revealing to watch them make their choice: Dolls? Or animals? Which animal? Very often the more gifted or more self-assertive children in a class will decide quite soon. The dreamy child or one who cannot make up his mind so well will follow suit. Thus there will be classes with predominately horses or lions or penguins, and so on. Yet no two of these will be alike. Each animal will be a character print of its maker. There will be phlegmatic lions and meek dragons. There is a terrier with a determined, self-assertive stride, walking with great self-reliance, made by a boy who, while being the shortest in his class, usually picked fights with boys much taller and stronger than he. There is a dog, with his head bent down, as if he had been scolded, made by a girl who came from a broken home. There is a camel with overlong, spindly legs, looking from a great height down onto the world and everything on it, made by a boy who was very gifted in mathematics, but at a loss whenever he had to cope with down-to-earth practical jobs like raking leavings or shoveling snow. However, his gift for mathematics made him feel quite superior and look down upon his classmates from the great height that he assumed. A bucking goat was made by a choleric boy, and a very "chatty" squirrel, together with a more placid one, characterize the two girls who made them.

None of these children aimed at expressing himself, but each one did.

While in the early grades the will-element in the children is mobilized in knitting and crocheting and in the upper grades thinking is predominately used in bookbinding, the making of stuffed animals and dolls is to a great extent accompanied by a strong element of feeling. There are of course various stages one goes through: first one has to decide what to do, then one has to settle down to the actual doing. The design has to be drawn and the pattern made from it. What pattern parts are needed in order to change a two-dimensional design into a three-dimensional animal? The problem is different in each case. After that, one chooses the fabric, cuts out, and begins to sew. Beginning with the pattern making, the steps are all technical until the sewing is finished and the form is turned inside out. This is usually accompanied by exclamations of surprise, and right away the new "pets" are given names. However, when the stuffing is done and all the details are finished—ears and tails put on, and eyes and noses—the joy is considerable.

I once asked a seventh-grader to lend me her stuffed animal for a school exhibit (she had done it the previous year but had not finished it on time for the previous school year's exhibit). She was very embarrassed and told me that she could not bring it; it was in no shape to be shown, for she had slept with it every night since she had taken it home.

Especially with the stuffed animals and dolls, one has a good opportunity to encourage the children to think of others and to use their toys as gifts. After all, we are dependent on others in every step of our daily life for food, clothing, and shelter, and it is important for us to learn to share and to give. This, too, is part of teaching crafts.

Seventh-graders continue to make projects for which they learn to develop patterns. They sew by hand and decorate with embroidery stitches. These projects are larger, more involved, mainly things to wear, like slippers and aprons, or things for the home, like place mats or pillow covers. They also begin to study the natural fibers: wool, cotton, linen, and silk. Man-made fibers are taken up in high school chemistry.

After having sewn by hand for several years and learned a variety of sewing and embroidery stitches, eighth-graders are now ready to learn how to use the sewing machine. Here treadle machines (if we can get them) are preferred to electric ones. One can control them with the coordination of one's body, very much like learning to ride a bicycle before using a motorcycle. It is also easier to understand and to repair the mechanism of a treadle than that of a motor-driven electric machine. Once the children have managed the coordination, they usually even prefer the treadle to an electric machine.

Their projects are simple tailored blouses for the girls and shirts for the boys. Commercial patterns are used so that the children learn to handle them. It is assumed that in their later life they will turn to commercial patterns whenever they need to sew a garment.

In looking back upon the crafts curriculum, there are certain "threads" that have been taken up and followed through the years: knitting, crocheting, sewing, embroidering, and so on. Why is it that we dealt consistently with threads or fabrics, as if they were the only things in the world that one could use for crafts?

We live in a fast-moving time in which we do not allow ourselves to go deeply and thoroughly into such activities as the crafts. We are surrounded by books that teach us "the easy way" or "the fast way" of doing something. It is characteristic that the greatest sign of appreciation nowadays given to a thing well done is: "But how long did it take you?" as if the assembly-line measure of time could be applied to an activity in which one is creatively involved. Can one really apply the time element to anything beyond the actual doing? Can one count the time that goes into the creative process itself?

If we think of all the aspects of the thread that the children have experienced, we can be sure that these children, when handling another material, such as clay or metal, will know quite naturally that these materials also have many aspects that have to be mastered, and that they will not lend themselves to dilettantic "quickies."

Crafts in the high school require an entirely different approach. While in the lower grades certain techniques were systematically developed, each year from now on has a certain theme. In the high school, the crafts teacher ought to be a specialist. Whatever is taught depends on his particular field.

The theme in the ninth grade is quite technical: how is it done? If pottery is taught, the children learn, for instance, to shape a cylindrical vase with coils, with evenly thick walls and straight, parallel sides. This is not easy and requires great sensitivity in their fingers. Throwing on the wheel is taught much later, if at all.

If dressmaking is done, the children will learn how to make the pattern for a simple garment and how to do the fitting. What body measurements does one have to take? What do the individual pattern parts look like? How are they to be assembled? What material would lend itself to a particular design?

If cabinetwork is done, the children will learn to make the working drawing of, for instance, a simple table or stool, how to cut the parts by hand, how to join them, and so on.

One could make reed-baskets or netted hammocks or simple bands, woven with tablets or on an Inkle loom. Weaving, like all other crafts, is introduced at a time when the children are ready to understand the whole process. In weaving, this process includes the setting up of a loom.

The theme for the tenth grade is teamwork. If dressmaking was taught in the ninth grade, the students can now, as a team, design and carry out costumes for a play, or work together on stage settings as a continuation of their woodworking course.

In anticipation of the bookbinding in the junior and senior years, some groups will also learn lettering in the tenth grade. This will enable them, after having bound their own books with blank pages, to letter and illustrate the poems that they have written or that they have been encouraged to collect in their class on English literature.

Juniors and seniors do bookbinding. Why bookbinding? This seems to be such an outdated craft. Why would a school that prides itself in being modern choose bookbinding as the culmination of its twelve years of crafts teaching? People who ask this question ought to take the time to bind a book themselves. They would soon find out in how many ways this craft will help young people not only on their way into college but on into life.

The various steps in bookbinding require careful planning. Their sequence is quite logical, and this logic must be understood. One must also know and understand the materials involved, their quality and character. There are on the market different kinds of cardboard, paper, and glue. What choices do I make for the project that I am planning? What do I use, and where and when? One has to be patient, to work with great precision, and to be able to think, particularly with one's fingertips.

When paste is brushed on paper, the paper will curl up. A newcomer to the trade will think he has to counteract this curling as fast and effectively as he can. Gradually he will realize that the paper acts just like a naughty child and he will learn to wait until the "tantrum" is over and the paper has relaxed, which it will have done after a while. It can then be handled without difficulties.

With its precision, inner discipline, and logic, bookbinding is, as a rule, a favorite craft among students. They even come frequently during college vacation to bind a book or to look nostalgically around the shop. This can well be understood if one also understands the human aspect of the craft. Bookbinding has a balancing quality in common with most other crafts. Because of this, many people who do strenuous thinking during the day pursue crafts hobbies in their leisure time.

Marty, a senior, came one day, in the late afternoon, to ask whether she would be permitted to work on her bookbinding project. She needed badly to do just that now, as she

Box, spoon and fork made by fifth grade students

had been preparing for the next day's mathematics tests and was all tense and tired in her head. "To work with my fingers is the only way to become human again," she said.

Competition has no place in our school system. Children are encouraged to do their best. However, their best has nothing to do with other children's best. Some children are strong intellectually and others artistically. We are not striving toward specialization but rather toward balancing, toward developing well-rounded human beings. The weaker points need to be strengthened, not the strong ones.

Paul was a brilliant intellectual. In bookbinding he understood very well what he had to do. Yet he was incapable of cutting even two pieces of cardboard to equal sizes, with four right angles to each piece. Roger was a kind, friendly, very practical boy, academically a poor student, but his hands worked like magic: everything he made was very accomplished. Paul would never have been able to bind a book without Roger helping and watching over every step of his work. Both boys complemented each other. It did Paul a lot of good not always to be first, and Roger needed just that situation in which he could give and help. Here the best academic student depended on the poorest.

So far we have dealt with various aspects of teaching crafts through the grades, yet we have not yet touched upon the aspect of design. The importance of design— dealing with the choice of material, form, color, and decoration in relation to the project— cannot be emphasized enough.

Here again there is nothing arbitrary about designing a project. Frank Lloyd Wright, the famous American architect, once said, "A design must be of a thing, not on it." What does that mean? The design is meant to enhance the character of an object in a qualitative way.

We need to know how and where the object is to be used in order to determine its form and decoration. Each object has a gesture entirely its own. A place mat, for instance, is a mat, confining the area on which all objects are placed that are needed by one person for eating. Its gesture means to say: this is my area, my place! If I want to decorate this place mat, the gesture of the decoration will, in a way, express this confinement. I will not want to put a design, for example, on an area that will be covered by an object, nor will I put it between myself and those objects.

A bag that hangs down and is filled with things is obviously closed at the bottom where it is also heavy with its contents. And it is open and lighter at the top. This can be expressed both in form and color: heavier, darker colors and closed form at the bottom, open form and lighter colors toward the top.

A belt is meant to run around the middle of our body, and the design on it will show this by being symmetrical in a horizontal way.

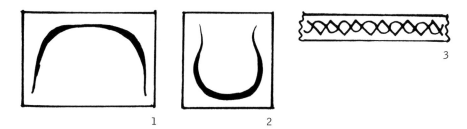

Gesture and actual design are not identical. The gesture is only meant to give the general theme, but within this theme there is ample room for individual imagination.

Colors have an objective and subjective side. In a subjective way I can say, " I like red," or, "I do not like red." But apart from this subjective approach, red also has an objective character of its own: it is aggressive. That is why it is used in advertising and in traffic. Yellow has more the tendency to ray out and blue has a more humble nature—it is enveloping, withdrawing. But of course all colors are bound to change and compromise, depending on the other colors they are associated with and on the general theme of the object on which they are used. The choice of a color scheme depends of course also on the individual child's personality.

I was once teaching form drawing in a class that I had never taught before. I did not know the children. I had brought with me a stack of construction paper in many colors, suggesting that each child choose the color that he liked best. While I was preoccupied

Snail made by a sixth grade student

with handing out the papers, a little boy asked me to give him a gray sheet. Without looking at him, I suggested that he take a red crayon for his drawing, thinking that red would show up well on the gray surface. Only then did I look at the boy and was struck by his terrified expression. I had not realized that he was a little introvert and therefore needed blue. When I then suggested to him a blue crayon, a smile went over his face, accompanied by a sigh of relief.

Throughout the twelve grades, the children are guided to create useful and beautiful colors. But the real purpose of crafts is to involve the whole child: head, heart, and hands, in order to develop all his potentialities.

APPRECIATIVE THINKING WITH SPECIAL REFERENCE TO THE TEACHING OF MATHEMATICS

Amos Franceschelli

The following article is an expanded version of an address given to the parents of the Rudolf Steiner School in New York City some years ago. One or two items are "dated," but not, in fact, outdated. The last paragraph (part 3) may be read first to avoid possible misconception in reading parts 1 and 2.

1

Many years ago, when I was doing graduate work in mathematics, a fellow student put a question to me that has remained with me since. As we were walking together one day in friendly conversation, he said, "Tell me, why are botanists so much nicer to get along with than mathematicians?"

When we met again after three decades of separation—he is a member of the mathematics department at one of our state universities and author of several significant professional books—I reminded him of his question.

He said, "Yes, tell me, why?"

Part of my answer—predicated, to be sure, on a quantum of implied truth in his question—was and is this: inherent in the study of mathematics today there is an element that makes for conceit. Do not misunderstand me. I do not mean that all mathematicians are conceited. I mean that the study of mathematics, especially in the higher echelons—stressing as it must a genius for analysis and abstraction, intellectual self-sufficiency, the possibility of perfect achievement, and an almost Jehovah-like power to create concepts and systems, together with the extraordinary role the subject plays in shaping our technological civilization—somehow tends to encourage the element of latent, unconscious self-conceit we are all born with.

This, in turn, can easily blend into an aspect of life that I would call "the critical attitude." We look around us, often enough, with a critical eye. We spot right away weaknesses and flaws—in a man, in a painting, in a nation, in the world. We think critically.

Now, critical thinking is an important and valuable faculty in man. It must be part of the school's effort to develop this faculty in its students. For critical thinking means a searching, fact-finding, discriminating kind of thinking. But it can also mean—especially if coupled with the element of unconscious conceit that I mentioned before—a negative, fault-finding, barren kind of thinking.*

Therefore, I believe it is no less the task of a school to cultivate the positive, balancing counterpart to this: namely, *appreciative thinking*. This indeed, has been an aim inherent in Waldorf education since its inception.

Let me illustrate, in brief.

Critical thinking, of a certain kind, looks at past civilizations and says, "How primitive! How naïve! How slow! Look at us today. . . ." Appreciative thinking, looking at past civilizations, might say, "How different! How interesting! We have wonderful new powers and insights today that they did not have. What powers and insights might they have had that today are lost to us?"

Critical thinking might look at Pythagoras (born about 57 B.C.), at his discovery and presumed proof of the famous theorem that bears his name, and say, "Quite a man, Pythagoras! A great discovery he made. But it is true, how silly! I guess he could not overcome the prejudices of his age. If I discovered a theorem, it's my own ingenuity I would thank for it!" Appreciative thinking, looking at the same, might say, "Strange—why should he and his times have indulged in such a whim? Or why should such a 'whim' have been attributed to him? Is there something more there than meets the eye? How did the Greeks experience mathematical concepts? How did they experience knowledge? What transformation may have occurred in man's consciousness and mode of experience over the centuries?"

Again, critical thinking, looking at some of the antics of modern youth,** might say, "How irresponsible! How futile!" Appreciative thinking, looking at the same, might say, "What hungers move these young people to act as they do? What nourishment can I bring them? What firm, new steps are needed?"

* That the botanist and the naturalist are less prone to this than the mathematician is an intriguing thesis that I leave unfinished here.
** See prefatory note.

If I were asked to describe, more specifically, the qualities of appreciative thinking, as I see it, I could list a number of them as follows:

Appreciate thinking seeks to be receptive or open—without lacking discrimination.
It seeks to be sensitive—without being morbid.
It seeks to be positive—without being Pollyannaish.
It seeks to be plastic—without being flabby.
It seeks to be mobile—without being restless or aimless.
It is aware of the wholeness of things in which we move and seek some ultimate harmony—without being blind to the role of conflict in life.
It is imaginative—without being fantastic.
It is truth seeking—without being sectarian.

And, in fact, it includes critical thinking, as the day includes day and night. All the above are, of course, ideal goals—but worth moving toward. I said before that the cultivation of appreciative thinking is an aim in all our teaching. Let me give a number of captioned examples in what follows, in more or less concentrated form, with special reference to mathematics at various levels in our twelve-grade school.

2

1. The Introduction of Number: The Whole and the Parts. The very introduction to number and to arithmetic operations in the first grade in our schools is associated with a primary experience of the whole that nourishes the faculty under discussion. I quote Mr. Harwood, former teacher at Michael Hall, England, who writes: "It will make a great difference to the tendency of the child's thinking for the rest of his life whether you fill the child's mind with the idea that 1 and 1 and 1 makes 3, or whether you start with 3 and break it up into parts. Ultimately and logically, the first leads to the idea that the universe is composed of atoms. The second, the grasping of the whole before the parts, is the way of imagination and leads to the view that it is only the whole that gives meaning and existence to the parts."* This is a somewhat bald assertion. Reflect a moment,

* A. C. Harwood, *The Recovery of Man in Childhood* (London: Hodder and Stoughton, 1958).

however, on the following. An ant crawling on the walls of a brick house, or a termite passing from beam to beam in it, no matter how thoroughly the one might tick off each brick or the other digest each beam, will never in this way gain conception of the edifice as such (I posit, of course, an "intelligent ant" and an "intelligent termite"). For it is the unifying idea of house, its primary wholeness in the architect's mind, that precedes and directs the gathering and collocation of bricks and beams and gives them meaningful reality as a habitation. Reflect on this, and you will begin to sense the importance of the point in question. But I do not propose here to expand the example, which I may have occasion to do another time.

2. First Prelude to Euclid: Movement and Form. Again, the first introduction to mathematical curves in our school, in one sense, is the living experience of "running them out," on the playground, on the floor of the eurythmy room, in the classroom itself. Concepts emerge, as it were, like salt crystals from a solution, form the prior, living fluid of an activity—that activity, precisely, in which they are operatively present. Thus, in an early grade, the teacher might have four children stand at the four corners of a large square chalked on the floor and, at a given signal, let the children move in response to the strong speaking of a verse—for instance:

In four directions we go forth:
*WEST—and SOUTH—and EAST—and NORTH!**

Each child leaves his or her corner for the next, as another child runs up to it, turns, and continues in rapid, rhythmic, right-angled succession. (The much later development of the geometric concept of a square is a story of its own.) Again, in the eurythmy lessons of the lowest grades, for instance, the children run such forms as circles, triangles, squares, pentagons, spirals, and figures of eight. Not, to be sure, in deference to geometric goals, but as related to the flow and pattern of eurythmy movement. Yet there is involved here, too, a live incubation of concepts that will come later (the class teacher will see to it that they do come later, at the proper moment, clearly formulated). At the same time, there is an element of social awareness in running through a form in a group, yielding the right place at the right time to your neighbor, which fosters an organ of sensitiveness for the acknowledgment of others—an essential ingredient in appreciative thinking.

3. Transformations in Geometry: The Triangle and the Trefoil. Mathematics, especially geometry, is all too often associated in our minds with rigidity, fixity, or form. Yet the

* From the notebooks of Dorothy Harrer, class teacher, Rudolf Steiner School, New York City, 1941–1971.

Geometric drawing by a sixth grade student

concepts and experience of mathematical transformation is inherent in the subject and of capital importance at all levels, for the sake of the subject itself and for the special purpose we are discussing. For instance, in studying the triangle as part of geometry proper in the sixth or seventh grade, we can do the following. Draw on the board, and have the children draw (construct) on their papers, a large equilateral triangle ABC, with its three medians, AP, BQ, and CR, meeting in a central point O. Divide each side into the same (even) number of parts, say twelve, all of which could be numbered, as shown in figure 1. Connect the center carefully by straight lines with each of the 36 points. Ask the children to imagine themselves standing one at each point of division (on a correspondingly large triangle, six in all, each of them facing exactly toward the center). Now tell them something like this: "Suppose that the size of the triangle is such that the distance from the foot of the median R to the center is 6 feet, i.e., RO = 6 feet; and the same, for each one of you is two feet. At this moment an eagle flying overhead would see you lined up in the form of a triangle, thirteen (!) on each straight side, all facing O. When I say GO, let everyone take one natural step forward in the direction you are facing–that is, toward O, and stop. Ready? GO! Now everyone has moved in a straight line two feet toward the center. How would you be lined up?" Give the children time to imagine this before you carry out the construction on the board (to scale), or before the children do it on paper by locating the new position or points with the help of a compass.

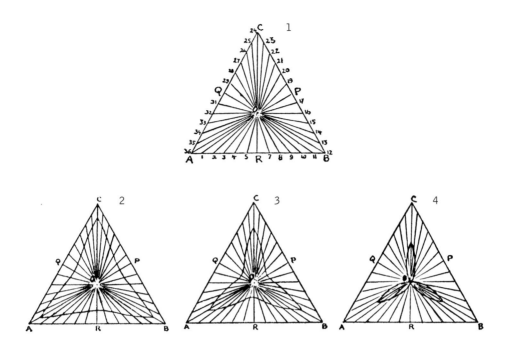

The rectilinear figure has been transformed into a symmetric figure bounded by three curvilinear arcs, as in figure 2. Continue in a similar way, and have the children "move in" toward O one more step (two feet, or another third of RO) and stop. What will the shape of the formation be now? (Imagine it.) See figure 3. Again, move two more feet, six feet in all now, or a length equal to RO, from each of the original points of division on the sides. What shape do the new positions, the new points, describe now? A three-leaved form, where threefold axial symmetry and closed curvilinear leaflets please the eye and intrigue the mind (figure 4).

The whole process—properly developed and carried out with the children—lies within the context of simple, precise mathematical laws and fosters a plastic, metamorphic quality in us that again nourishes the faculty I have called appreciative thinking.*

(The mathematical reader will have noticed that we have been dealing here with a triple generation of a curve, or arc of a curve, known as the conchoid of Nicomedes. It plays an interesting role in mathematics, especially in connection with one of the three

* I have sketched only a first development of this transformation. It admits extensions and variations, which I omit here. Also, the use of color at this level should be encouraged. How all this is done with the children is of the essence. The transformation was originally introduced into our schools, I believe, by Dr. Hermann von Baraville. See also his booklet, *Geometric Drawing and the Waldorf School Plan*, Waldorf School Monographs (Englewood, N.J., 1967).

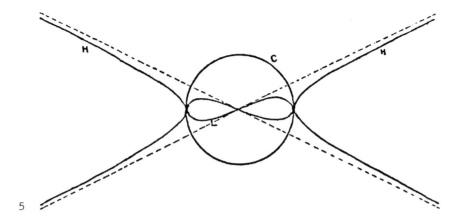

5

The hyperbola that lies in the "infinite world" outside the circle C is transformed by inversion (with respect to circle C) into the lemniscate contained in the "bounded world" inside the circle. This is an example of inversion in a plane. Inversion in three-dimensional space is based on a sphere.

famous problems of antiquity, the trisection of an angle. Thus, too, the opportunity is prepared to return to this curve in later years, and bring out its locus property, its trisection aspect, and historical overtones on a new level.)

3b. Transformations in Geometry: Inversion and Garden Globes. I shall not forbear here from mentioning another illustration in the teaching of mathematics where the transformation motif and its encouragement of a plastic, metamorphic, and even imaginative quality of thinking (but mathematically disciplined) is especially striking. I am referring to inversive geometry, of which the simplest elements are incorporated in a special main-lesson block on projective geometry (most intuitive and constructive) in the eleventh grade in our school. I cannot develop the concept of inversion within the limits of this article. But those who have met it and have worked with it can realize, perhaps, how in the possibility of transforming an infinite outer world into a bounded inner world (see figure 5), based on a clearly enunciated and relatively simple mathematical law, there is a source of excellent exercises for the disciplined education of more than one aspect of the thought power under discussion.

And having gone through such exercises in the proper manner, after the proper preparation, with the students, one can say to them: Do we not see a similar phenomenon when we look at a garden globe—in which the most distant cloud finds its counterpart by reflection within—or, by the same token, in all and every dewdrop in which the sun is reflected—or in the eyeball that images all things before it—or perhaps even in man who, in himself, condenses in thought and flesh the grandeur of the whole wide universe? We must be careful to circumscribe our concepts and analogies rightly, for the parallel is one of motif rather than equivalence (the law in the examples just given is not mathematically the same as for inversion, especially, of course, in the last one!). But such references are not extraneous and can be valuable.

4. Algebra: Equations, the Golden Rule, and Balance. In algebra, which seems so formless as compared with geometry (form does play a role in it, but in a subtler way), there are also many opportunities related to our purpose. Consider, for instance, the solving of a simple equation:

$$5x - 3 = 17$$

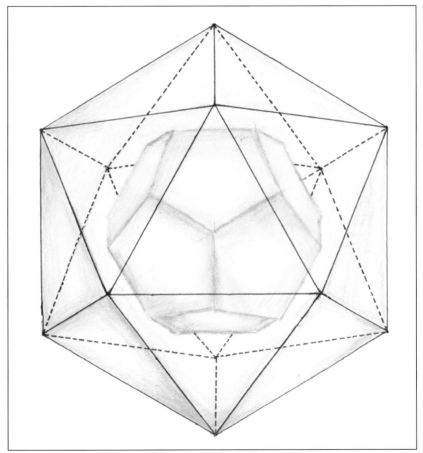

Drawing by an eighth grade student for a Geometry main lesson

From the outset (in the upper elementary grades) we associate with an equation the concept and experience of balance, of a perfectly balanced beam, say, resting on its fulcrum F:

$$5x - 3 = 17$$

F

and recognize the fundamental approach for solving it: we transform the two sides of the equation in such a way that we never destroy the balance (Golden Rule: "Do to one side what you do to the other," later formulated as axioms), until we isolate the x on the one side:

Step 1: add 3 to *both* sides: $5x - 3 + 3 = 17 + 3$ or $5x = 20$
Step 2: divide *both* sides by 5: $5x/5 = 20/5$ or $x = 4$

Somewhere along the line (not right away, but at some later time) this furnishes opportunity for various "incidental" dialogues with the class. For instance: an algebraic equation "is" a balance. A physical balance has a fulcrum. Where is the fulcrum in the equation? In the equals sign. Yes, but where is the fulcrum really as you work with the equation? Do you hold up the two sides with your hands? With what? With my mind. And where is the fulcrum there? "I" am the fulcrum. "I" am that which constantly holds up the equation so that it balances. . . . One need not press this "I am" reference too far. But one can develop other thought with it. For instance, where else do we find the phenomenon of balance? Yes, in a physical balance (we already know), in a lever. Where closer home? In ourselves on earth. Every moment that we stand or walk on our feet we are transformed just as I am, in front of you, into a life-size manikin, with articulated joints, and that it tried to move! It might take one or two jerky steps forward, then likely tumble to the floor. Yet look at me as I really am, a live man again: I wave my arms sideways, or lift high my right leg, or bend, or dance—and with every gesture I make, which would throw a wooden dummy off balance, I make an immediate muscular adjustment of some sort that enables me to preserve my balance through countless changing movements all the time. We are able, I am able, at every conscious moment of my life, to preserve a balance so delicate and versatile and wonderful that no mechanical robot, to my knowledge, so much as approximates it. (This could lead to other significant observations; for instance: what of a man in a swoon, or drunk, or dead? But we must be judicious with our "incidental" dialogues, for remember that we are teaching algebra.) It is enough to suggest or stimulate certain thoughts that are significantly related to the mathematical process we are teaching (the preservation of balance in an equation by "simultaneous adjustment" on both sides), at the proper moment, in the right way, without belaboring them. The student's thinking, I believe, is made more open, more aware, more mobile—that is, more appreciative—at least, a little impulse is given in that direction.

5. *Algebra: Mathematics and Reality—Two Solutions to a Quadratic Equation.* That human thought, and in particular mathematical thought (weightless, impalpable, even abstract to begin with) can take hold of the world around us (altogether weightful, palpable, concrete), and do so with remarkable concordance and effect, can be brought out in many ways, at many levels, and deepen the student's appreciation of its role. A striking illustration is afforded in the ninth grade when discussing the solution of a quadratic equation (such as $x^2 - 3x + 2 = 0$) for the first time. Up to this point, the student has solved many equations of the first degree, like the one explained in section 4 above, and found always exactly one answer, one root, as one might well expect. Now we meet the intriguing fact that an equation such as

$$x^2 - 3x + 2 = 0$$

has two answers, or two roots (in this case, x = 1 and x = 2). How can this be? To what kind of reality could this correspond? To leave this unanswered will leave a residue of conscious or unconscious discontent, even rebellion, in the student. One can meet this in a simple way. Right after learning (in the ninth grade) how to solve such an equation by factoring, and discovering the unexpected phenomenon of two solutions for the same equation, I have brought in a formula taken from physics that tells that the distance s through which a stone travels in t seconds when it is thrown vertically upward with an initial velocity of u feet per second, is:

$$s = ut - 16t^2$$

Now I put the question: In how many seconds will a stone thrown vertically up with a starting velocity of 48 feet per second reach a height of 32 feet above its starting point? If we substitute, we find

$$t^2 - 3t + 2 = 0$$

and solve (by factoring) to find that t = 1 second, or t = 2 seconds. How is this possible? Which is right, 1 second or 2 seconds?—The adult will probably know at once what to think of this. But I well remember the concentrated, puzzled, searching silence with which

An exercise in parallel lines

Drawing by an eleventh grade student for Projective Geometry

a class sought to fathom out the answer to the question—which is it, 1 second or 2 seconds?—while I stood in front of it tossing a piece of chalk to the ceiling and letting it fall back into my hand, while pointing to a position in midair that was supposed to represent a distance of 32 feet above my hand when it released the chalk. There was a prolonged silence while I kept tossing up the chalk and catching it again as it came down. Then, from the back of the room, a sudden voice: Both are right! One second and two seconds. Yes, the chalk reaches the 32-foot height 1 second after it is thrown, continues to its highest point, falls back, and reaches the same height again 2 seconds after it is thrown! There was, I believe, a general marveling, satisfied feeling when it was recognized. That mathematics should so beautifully "reflect" or "contain" the double truth of the real phenomenon! No wonder Einstein was intrigued to the end of his life, as I have read, by the fact that man can evolve a whole mathematical world from within—in an ivory tower, as it were—

and yet find such far-reaching correspondence or harmony of its results with the real world outside. (The same context, using the same formula as above, can be varied to give meaning to a negative solution, and, later, to imaginary solutions.)

6. From Chaos to Order. I take another illustration related to geometry, but in part also to arithmetic and algebra, in the upper elementary grades, which offers the opportunity to develop clear mathematical concepts and stimulate many-sided thought at the same time. It combines application of basic constructions (using straight-edge and compass) with a first study of quadrilaterals. Ask the class to draw any large (irregular) quadrilateral on a sheet of paper, one for each pupil, bisect the sides (emphasize care and accuracy!), then connect the successive midpoints of the sides by straight-line segments. Let them contemplate the results. In all cases, however "random" the original quadrilateral, we find a more ordered or well-balanced figure emerge within the irregular one: a *parallelogram*. (Allow the children time to be struck by this.) Now ask them to bisect each of the four angles of the parallelogram (again: care and accuracy), and look at the result. This time, an even more balanced, special figure appears: a *rectangle*. Once more, ask them to bisect the angles of the rectangle (care and accuracy!)—what is the result? The ultimate, regular quadrilateral: a *square*. The whole figure might look like this:

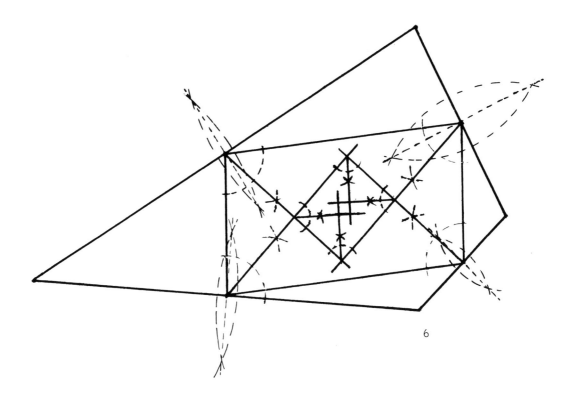

6

The children see how the emerging figures acquire an increasing quality of regularity—from quadrilateral to square—from randomness to order (to increasing order, of a certain kind!). The teacher must not fail, of course, to bring out the precise meaning of the various geometrical concepts involved in and related to the topic: polygon, regular polygon, quadrilateral, rhombus, parallelogram, rectangle, square, and so on. At the same time, an opportunity is afforded to point out the role of order (and different levels of order; see below and section 7) in the world, perhaps the role of both order and disorder. I well remember how one day in a seventh-grade lesson, I described some of the manifold rhythms and patterns that pervade the heavens, the earth, and man himself; and how one pupil, on the day following, when we were reviewing, raised her hand and said earnestly: "You told us about order and rhythm everywhere around us yesterday. But there is so much confusion in the world!" It was one of those special moments in the classroom that call upon the teacher's deepest resources to answer truly and meaningfully, particularly at that level. It was also possible, a little later, to hint at a greater riddle, perhaps—namely, that apparent disorder may hide a deeper kind of order—by utilizing arithmetic phenomena. Compare the following two number squares:

$$
\begin{array}{ccc}
1\ 2\ 3 & & 8\ 1\ 6 \\
4\ 5\ 6 & \text{and} & 3\ 5\ 7 \\
7\ 8\ 9 & & 4\ 9\ 2
\end{array}
$$

Which exhibits greater order at first blush? Surely the one on the left. Yet the reader will recognize that the right-hand square is a so-called magic square, in which each row, column, and diagonal adds up to 15, and thus in a sense possesses a higher kind of order than the order of the natural numbers in the first one. Somehow, in pointing this out—clearly, soberly, without false emphases, and without neglecting some of the genuine mathematical aspects—something is done to foster the power of unhobbled, searching, wide-ranging thinking in the child.

Note also the valuable background thus prepared for later grades, when the intuitively recognized geometric phenomena described above will be shown to be inherently necessary by logical proof; or when the formula for the sum of the first n terms of an arithmetic progression can be applied to magic squares as well as to more practical situations.

7. Geometry, Mathematical Symmetry, and Living Symmetry—Orders of Perfection. I take another example, this time from tenth-grade geometry. Symmetry is a property of many Euclidian figures—of regular polygons, for instance, and of circles. There are different kinds of symmetry (about a point, a line, a plane), which can be discussed at the proper time, beginning in the elementary grades. In tenth grade, as a marginal exercise—I mean, as a side trip away from the sterner path of demonstrative work—I have at times asked my students to draw individual patterns exhibiting axial symmetry based on a constructed background grid of concentric circles and evenly spaced diameters. For instance:

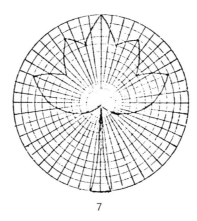

7

(This can be done even in color, it need not be a waste of time.) Again, a dialogue can be pursued with the class in connection with this. The leaf form you have drawn above had, at least in principle, perfect axial symmetry. Do the leaves of a natural tree also have axial symmetry? Yes, many of them, of a sort—but not "exact." Do you think any one actual leaf has the exact symmetry of the one you constructed? Probably not. What if a tree had all of its leaves exactly symmetrical like the one above, through perhaps of quite different form—would you think it more or less beautiful than a real tree? (Reflection.) Are the leaves of a tree less perfect than the one drawn? In one sense, yes; in another, no. They have another kind of perfection, perhaps a "higher" kind of symmetry. (One is reminded here of the concept of dynamic symmetry. The reader may feel moved to make critical comments about "beauty" and "subjective values." This is not the place, unfortunately, to enter into them.) The point is, however, that with a mathematical experience as a starting point, the students' thoughts have been stimulated into an appreciation and differentiation of qualities in the wider world around them and, perhaps, into a new awareness of questions as they contemplate the world. Experiencing and recognizing questions is the first step toward seeking and finding answers.

8a. The Computer and Barzun. The discussion of numeration systems with bases other than 10, especially of the binary system and, in connection with it or other topics, of modern computers, can lead to dialogues with the class especially relevant to our times and life and thus again promote perceptive and appreciative thinking. The question "Will 'electronic brains' ever take over or displace the human mind?" in some form or other has intrigued, amused, or bemused many minds. There are deep-reaching implications in the question. How the dialogue with the class proceeds must depend on the individuality of the teacher and on the maturity of the class. "What, essentially, is the sum total of a large computer's powers?" said an IBM engineer talking to a senior class in our school. "Two things: it can add 1 and 1, and it can choose between two paths in a circuit; only much faster than man." In this connection, Jacques Barzun's comment on computers is also relevant. We are overawed by computers, he said, which can do things far beyond the power of ordinary mortals; but so can every other machine worthy of the name, for instance, a corkscrew. It is not, however, a question of playing down or playing up computers, but of (1) understanding something of how they work and of their role in society today; and (2) stimulating many-sided, pertinent thought when the mathematical situation offers the adequate opportunity.

8b. The Computer, Anthropomorphism, and Clarity of Thought. In fact, there is, I believe, in the teaching of computer principles, a special opportunity to help the young mind awaken to clear thinking. I do not mean here only the fact that a computer program must be set up to yield the desired output on the basis of a cloudless mastery of process and detail. This kind of clarity is important but is relatively easy to achieve (up to a point). I mean, rather, a stripping away of fuzziness of meaning in the use of concepts and words. For instance, can the student, can we recognize unequivocally the difference between such statements as "The computer reads a card," or "The computer compares two numbers," or "The computer makes a logical decision," and the corresponding sentences for man: "Man reads a card," "Man compares two numbers," "Man makes a logical decision"? (In the first decade of computer popularity, the anthropomorphic language used in describing computer processes evoked speculative thrills about machines that think.) It is almost sufficient to point out, for our purpose, the difference between:

"The pen writes"   and   "The author writes."

Both of which are, of course, perfectly legitimate expressions. Or to furnish simple examples of machines that "compare" and "make logical decisions" (e.g., a ramp with two holes tandem, of different size, that select our small bearings and large bearings rolling down its incline). In a sense computers do exhibit "thinking power"—namely, in the same way any machine exhibits it by embodying some fragment of human thought that has been projected and constrained into it, or in the way a record player exhibits "musical power." In any case, the student's thinking can be stirred and helped to avoid one-sided spellboundedness.

9. Pattern Discovery and Variations on a Motif: The Chambered Nautilus. Pattern discovery is a significant aspect of mathematics, especially stressed in the reforms of the last two decades. This is a welcome emphasis for a number of reasons, including the fact that recognition of a pattern, and especially recognition of a motif in different contexts, surely promotes one quality of appreciative thinking. I mention an example of this in brief, taken from algebra in high school. The study of arithmetic progressions and geometric progressions offers a fine opportunity for exhibiting a theme at various levels and in various ways. Bare reference must suffice here. We find one or the other of these progressions, or both, at work:

i.   in numbers and in their logarithms, and hence in the slide rule;
ii. in the chromatic scale of well-tempered tuning (cf. a piano);
iii. in astronomy, in "Bode's Law" for planetary distances;
iv. in biology, in the multiplication of cells;
v.   in banking, in compound interest;
vi. in geometry, in two basic kinds of spirals, the Archimedean spiral (figure 8a) and the logarithmic spiral (figure 8b);
vii. in the shells of snails and many other shells. To show the students, say, the cross section of a chambered nautilus, in which the logarithmic spiral (and hence a geometric progression) secretly and overtly informs the beauty of the shell, should not be considered a merely decorative act.

8A   8B

Other cases could be found. The above "variations on a theme," again presented at the right time and not overdone, foster, I believe, the power under discussion. And what should prevent us, as we recapitulate, at the close of these variations, from reading in class Oliver Wendell Holmes's memorable poem "The Chambered Nautilus," before passing on to the next algebraic topic?

10. The Ikaya-Seki Comet and Newton. A fine example. Historical references, historical perspectives, can do much to foster appreciative thinking. When, for instance, the Ikaya-Seki comet appeared in the night skies in October-November 1965, there was a special opportunity, above all in the math classes, to speak a bit of mathematical laws in the universe, of circular, elliptical, and parabolic orbits, of Ptolemy, Copernicus, Kepler,

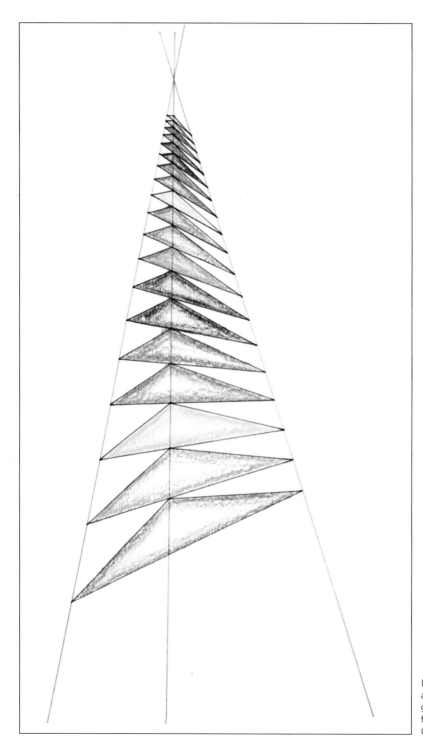

Drawing by
an eleventh
grade student
for Projective
Geometry

and Newton; and in particular, after describing something of the greatness of Newton, who is considered one of the foremost geniuses in mathematics and science, to bring to the students' attention two quotations by Newton himself.

. . . If I have seen farther than others, it is by standing on the shoulder of giants.*
. . . I don't know what I may seem to the world, but as to myself, I seem to have been only as a boy playing on the seashore, and diverting myself in now and then finding a smoother pebble or a prettier shell than the ordinary, while the great ocean of truth lay all undiscovered before me.

3

I have tried to give some illustrations of how, at various levels, an effort can be made through mathematics to develop a faculty that I have called appreciative thinking. It is a faculty that, I am convinced, is a vital element for genuine success—in college, in life, when alone with our cares and problems, when working as part of a team. Notice that I have said "through mathematics." You will not think that what I have described here is the content or main trunk of our mathematics. The content and main trunk is the substance, the insights, the techniques, the logic, of arithmetic, algebra, geometry, trigonometry, projective geometry, elementary functions, and so on, described in the curriculum and aimed at preparation for college as well as growth and life. The other is an incidental by-product of method, as far as the method is successful. But it is an incidental-deliberate by-product in all our subjects, or should be. The examples could be multiplied. Many of them arose as spontaneous "asides" at the right moment. None will prove fruitful if merely imitated. In any case, I hope that what I have given affords a glimpse of a pedagogical perspective that we all hold before us, at least as an ideal, and that can be pursued also through mathematics.

* Another version of this quotation reads: "If I have seen farther than Descartes . . ." but the essential meaning remains.

The Schooling of Imagination Through Literature and Composition

Christy Barnes

What is the importance of imagination today?

Has it any relation to practical life, to industry, to social conditions, to reality? If so, can we educate it? Can it be cultivated and trained?

Education is and has for a long time been oriented toward informing the mind and training it to respond to facts and problems as speedily, logically, and accurately as possible. Our schools are based on the indisputable premise that intellectual powers and access to information are necessary and important for life and progress, and that their efficiency can be improved.

Many of us look upon imagination as a pleasant and admirable embellishment to cultural life. But there have been and are men—writers, scientists, statesmen, planners of all kinds—who say that without imagination we cannot foresee, organize, or originate what is needed for the future.

The relationship of education to intellect and to imagination is one of the most fundamental problems of the new generation.

At the beginning of our age, men such as Emerson, Goethe, and Tolstoy were aware that a one-sided trend was developing, especially in the field of science. In his essay "Modern Science" Tolstoy says,

> Our science, in order to become science and to be really useful instead of harmful to humanity, must first of all renounce its experimental method, which causes it to consider as its business merely the study of what exists, and return it to the only wise and fruitful understanding of science, according to which its subject is the investigation of how men should live.

With this statement he adds to the scientist's newly won competence in objective observation two other powers: those of imaginative foresight and of moral responsibility.

> The eye of the naturalist must have a scope like nature itself, a susceptibility to all impressions, alive to the heart as well as to the logic of creation,

says Emerson in the chapter on literature in his English Traits, in which he makes a complaint similar to Tolstoy's. He observes, incipient in England, for which he has a deep admiration, a tendency that has taken root in much of specialized science and education throughout the world today.

> But English science puts humanity to the door. It lacks the connection which is the test of genius. The science is false by not being poetic. It isolates the reptile and the mollusk it assumes to explain; whilst reptile and mollusk only exist in system, in relation. The poet only sees it as an inevitable step in the path of the Creator. But in England one hermit finds this fact, and another finds that, and lives and dies ignorant of its value. There are great expectations . . . but for the most part science in England is out of its loyal alliance with morals, and it is a void of imagination and free play of thought as conveyancing. It stands in strong contrast with the genius of the Germans, those semi-Greeks [Emerson had been studying Goethe] who love analogy, and by means of their height of view, preserve their enthusiasm and think for Europe.

The romantic poets, Wordsworth, Shelley, Keats, created their own peaceful revolution and cultivated imagination as "the only means of grasping the unseen": the unseen forces that penetrate into and make sense of the seen and without a knowledge of which we can have no mastery over the visible, practical world, without which we treat symptoms, not causes.

We today have educated our thinking to become accurate, sharp, and objective, and, we hope, to accord with reality. One of the most effective training grounds in this achievement has been that aspect of nature that can be weighed and measured, that which is dead.

Goethe and Thoreau, however, were not content with this. For Thoreau, a plant torn out of its home and pressed between pages was a half-lie. These men were pioneers with whom we are only just beginning to catch up. They observed the world whole: the qualitative with the quantitative; living, changing forms, each in relationship to the others; and within the multiplicity and diversity of phenomena they also observed laws, such laws as change flower to fruit, grub to butterfly, child to man. Can we, like them, school the image-forming eye upon the objective, animate analogies and metamorphoses of nature? The following are some of a teacher's attempts in this direction.

Ask a student to look at a leaf, the stem branching away from the twig, the veins from the stem, the tinier tributaries angling out from these into the "watershed" of leafy substance. Let him feel his way with eye and heart into the gestures of eager, child-like trust with which a leaf lifts into the sun. Let him observe intently until vagueness and boredom vanish in the face of his absorption in these subtleties of living imagery.

Then turn his attention to the great analogy-creating powers of nature. Let him follow in his mind the image of a river, from whose central stem (cut by the currents as they flow downward to the sea) branches extend up into the foothills and multiply into the streams of mountain watersheds. The river system is unlike the leaf in size and substance. Its webbing of field and rock cannot sail on the wind. Its current flows in the contrary direction. Nevertheless, these two images, these two patterns, overlaid one upon the other, have certain congruence. This congruence the poet calls metaphor. The leaf is a more individualized and tinier river basin, lifted and given independence by the air, the river basin a giant, continental leaf.

Where the shapes or qualities of two or even several images converge upon or overlap one another, like the intersecting arcs on a surveyor's map, X marks the spot where the treasure is buried. And the treasure? An unseen idea or law, in this case a law governing the way in which a flowing substance penetrates a more solid one with the greatest possible economy: a branching that we see made visible in leaf and lung, in blood vessels and the map of continents, in the veins of rocks: an irrigation or circulation. Imagination, the faculty that can grasp the invisible law or idea, unifies and reveals meaning in the seemingly chaotic and senseless scene. It sees the connections between water, traffic and blood systems, between sleep and death, the organism of man and of human society, microcosm and macrocosm. Through analogy we become the surveyors and treasure seekers of the known world.

It was this kind of imagination that informed Thoreau when he wrote in Walden in his chapter "Spring":

> Few phenomena gave me more delight than to observe the forms which thawing sand and clay assume in flowing down the sides of a deep cut in the railroad. . . . Innumerable little streams overlap and interlace one with another, exhibiting a sort of hybrid product, which obeys half way the law of currents, and half way that of vegetation. As it flows it takes the form of sappy leaves or vines, making heaps of pulpy sprays; you are reminded of coral, of leopard's paws or birds' feet, of brains or lungs or bowels, and excrements of all kinds. It is truly . . . a sort of architectural foliage. . . . I am affected as if in a peculiar sense I stood in the laboratory of the Artist who made the world and me. . . . No wonder that the earth expresses itself outwardly in leaves, it so labors with the idea inwardly. The atoms have already learned this law and are pregnant with it. The overhanging leaf sees here its prototype. *Internally*, whether in the globe or animal body, it is a moist, thick

lobe, a word especially applicable to the liver and lungs and the leaves of fat . . . *externally*, a dry thin leaf. . . . The feathers and wings of birds are still drier, thinner leaves. Thus, also, you pass from the lumpish grub in the earth to the airy, fluttering butterfly. The very globe continually transcends and translates itself, and becomes winged in its orbit.

Here Thoreau not only points to analogies in nature, but traces the forward, upward tendency of creation. Thoreau continues:

> Even ice begins with delicate crystal leaves. . . . The whole tree itself is but one leaf, and rivers are still vaster leaves whose pulp is intervening earth, and towns and cities are the ova in their axils. . . .

> The Maker of this earth but patented a leaf. . . . There is nothing inorganic. . . . The earth is not a mere fragment of dead history, stratum upon stratum like the leaves of a book, to be studied by geologists and antiquaries chiefly, but living poetry like the leaves of a tree, which precede flower and fruit—not a fossil earth, but a living earth; compared with whose great central life all animal and vegetable life is merely parasitic.

In such a passage Thoreau touches upon the natural metaphors and metamorphoses composed by "the Artist in his laboratory." A teacher can do no worse than set his pupil's feet upon a path along which he may explore these "ideas" with which "the earth labors."

Let him have a student choose some theme, the sun, a leaf, the process of breathing, and trace it through the kingdoms of nature—mineral, plant, animal, man, from stone to star—perhaps through the elements of earth, water, air, and fire. Let him see how it works in the human eye and in thought. He cannot help, then, but come upon the embodied metaphor instilled there by that "Artist who made the world and me." What he writes afterward, whether he is gifted or not, will be of the stuff of imagination and the stuff of truth also, if he is rightly guided to respect accuracy.

It is up to the teacher to help a student to distinguish between illusion and "real imagination." One means of doing this is to guide him methodically through three steps in the imaginative process: first, the very accurate observation and reproduction of an image; second, the tracing of carefully authenticated analogies to this image, through which he is led to recognize the fundamental law that creates their congruence. Let him relate microcosm and macrocosm: "See," like Blake, "a world in a grain of sand." Take any small object, nature-made, and read from it its greater counterpart, its secret embodiment of large in little. Choose a nut, a shell, a drop of dew, the whorls of a fingerprint, a plank of wood. The following, taken from compositions by high school students, were written for such assignments:

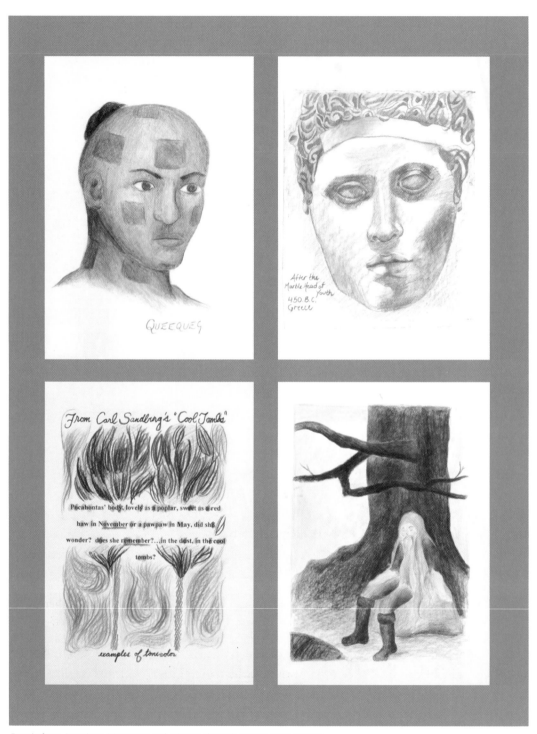

Panels from American Literature and History through Poetry main lessons

SNOWDROP

The snowdrop appears in a pile of damp, rotten, black leaves as soon as the snow recedes. Its form is deceptively delicate: one would never believe that beneath this gently drooping, curved head and graceful leaves sweeping upward, there burns an indomitable spirit which holds it alive through the winter's last fierce frosts and storms. The snowdrop's head is pure white, silky and almost waxen in texture; it curls downward from the smooth green stem, sheltered by strong, upright leaves. It has no smell, as far as I know; it is always found in clusters of modest blooms. As spring finally comes, the three petals and calyx leaves open into a luminous six-pointed star which shines in triumph for a while; then it fades, giving way to the brighter, colorful crocuses and daffodils.

The snowdrop is aptly named; in a way, it brings a drop of winter and re-embodies it in a redeeming form. It is as if, out of the wild whiteness, one drop has been reborn in the form of a flower. When the snowdrop opens, the six-petaled star reminds one of a snowflake, which also, in a way, redeems snow and frozen earth, but it also is the first to herald the approach of its brethren in a new spring.

M.M.

THE GEODE

I have often marveled at the skeleton of the earth, and have had occasion to see some of the most beautiful members of its massy system. . . .

On splitting open a plain, pock-marked global rock, one usually encounters its constituents, sometimes arranged in delightful patterns, but on the whole, uninteresting in their actual appearance. A geode, however, is a hollow sphere, the inside lined by the most perfect crystals: droplets of sunshine trapped within the living stone and peering at one another. The many facets reflect a light which is dazzling under their source, the sun. The geode seems truly a symbol of the universe: serene purity enclosed and encrusted in "ordinary" matter, its calyx.

I am always looking for a man who is a geode, a man who may look like any other, but whose soul is so pure and ordered that he blazes with a radiance and thereby activates the minds of those who chance to perceive this inner "crystal array." Such men are rare, and before a geode is found, numerous rocks must be opened; but the discovery of a geode, and of such a man, is an exciting triumph and an occasion which must change the discoverer forever.

D.S.

A teacher may also investigate with his students the laws of metamorphosis: how an entity is always in flux, maintaining its essence yet radically changing its form. Let a student follow the seed to sprout; the bud, flower, and fruit to see. Let him match this sequence with that of egg to caterpillar; cocoon to butterfly to egg. Let him see how the activities of a child are other than those of an adult: how in the capacities of a growing boy from the wriggling larva of imitation through the cocoon of dreaming bursts at last the winged creature—thought.

The third step in imagination is based upon the study of such actualities, and is the discovery of that fire that creates and shapes new images, out of which may evolve poems, music, all works of art, inventions, or social reforms. Schooled by reality and respect for truth during the first two steps, a man will hopefully produce a new creation and introduce it to the world with a sense of its fitting, constructive relation to nature and to society as a whole.

In this third step, the student poet must "digest" his observations, even destroy them in the fires of his being, if need be, as he destroys the food he eats, and then re-create the nourishing substance into a new organism of colorful, musical poetic form. For a poem is a thought become color, form, and music—or, music, color, and form become thought.

The Venerable Bede said of the Anglo-Saxon poet Caedmon: "And like a clean animal ruminating" he absorbed the Bible stories he was told and "gave them forth again" like milk "in sweet verse."

Of these wondrous processes of making metaphor and poetic composition, George MacDonald has this tiny fairy tale to tell in his *Phantastes:*

> Once as I passed by a cottage, there came out a lovely fairy child, with two wondrous toys, one in each hand. The one was the tube through which the fairy-gifted poet looks when he beholds the same thing everywhere; the other that through which he looks when he combines into new forms of loveliness those images of beauty which his own choice has gathered from all regions wherein he has traveled. Round the child's head was an aureole of emanating rays. As I looked at him in wonder and delight, round crept from behind me a something dark, and the child stood in my shadow. Straightway he was a commonplace boy, with a rough, broad-brimmed straw hat, through which brim and sun shone from behind. The toys he carried were a multiplying-glass and a kaleidoscope. I sighed and departed.

One can make clear and alive to the students the responsibility of the artist (and scientist) by reading with them another excerpt from George MacDonald, who might almost be called the Novalis of English literature. C. S. Lewis acknowledged him to be his master, and whoever knows MacDonald's gem of a fairy tale *The Golden Key*, or has read and reread his *Princess and Curdie* and other children's books, comes to realize that here is a master indeed. With him, you step into a world of such truth- and wisdom-imbued imagination that it all but eclipses many a work of more acknowledged fantasy.

From Preface to
*THE LIGHT PRINCESS,
AND OTHER FAIRY TALES*

. . . Some thinkers would feel sorely hampered if at liberty to use no forms but as existed in nature, or to invent nothing save in accordance with the laws of the world of the senses; but it must not therefore be imagined that they desire escape from the region of law. Nothing lawless can show the least reason why it should exist, or could at best have more than a semblance of life.

The natural world has its laws, and no man must interfere with them in the way of presentment any more than in the way of use, but they themselves may suggest laws of other kinds, and man may, if he pleases, invent a little world of his own, with its own laws; for there is that in him which delights in calling up new forms—which is the nearest, perhaps, he can come to creation. When such forms are new embodiments of old truths, we call them products of the Imagination. When they are mere inventions, however lovely, I should call them the work of the Fancy: in either case, Law has been diligently at work.

His world once invented, the highest law that comes next into play is, that there shall be harmony between the laws by which the new world has begun to exist; and in the process of his creation, the inventor must hold by those laws. The moment he forgets one of them, he makes the story, by its own postulates, incredible. To be able to live a moment in an imagined world, we must see the laws of its existence obeyed. Those broken, we fall out of it. The imagination in us, whose exercise is essential to the most temporary submission to the imagination of another, immediately, with the disappearance of Law, ceases to act.

Imagine the gracious creatures of some childlike region of Fairyland talking either Cockney or Gascon! Would not the tale, however, lovely begun, sink at once to the level of the burlesque—of all forms of literature the least worthy? A man's inventions may be stupid or clever but if he does not hold by the laws of them, or if he make one law jar with another, he contradicts himself as an inventor, he is no artist. He does not rightly consort his instruments, or he tunes them in different keys. The mind of man is the product of live Law; it thinks by law, it dwells in the midst of law, it gathers from law its growth; with law, therefore, can it alone work to any result. Inharmonious, unconsorting ideas will come to a man, but if he try to use one of such, his work will grow dull, and he will drop it for mere lack of interest. Law is the soil in which alone beauty will grow; beauty is the only stuff in which Truth can be clothed; and you may, if you will, call Imagination the tailor that puts the pieces of them together, or perhaps at most works their button-holes. Obeying law, the maker works like his creator; not obeying law, he is such a fool as heaps a pile of stones and calls it a church.

In the moral world it is different: there a man may clothe in new forms, and for them employ his imagination freely, but he must invent nothing. He may not, for any purpose, turn its laws upside down. He must not meddle with the relations of live souls. The laws of the spirit of man must hold, alike in this world and in any world he may invent. It were no offence to suppose a world in which everything repelled instead of attracted, the things around it; it would be wicked to write a tale representing a man it called good as always doing bad things; or a man it called bad as always doing good things: the notion itself is absolutely lawless. In physical things a man may invent; in moral things he must obey— and take their laws with him into his invented world as well.

Perhaps most important of all, such exercises in imagination may provide a sense of meaningfulness and worthwhileness of life that can reach in a healing way to the roots of adolescent disturbance, bitterness, and withdrawal, as Olive Schreiner describes in her novel of the conflicts of youth, *The Story of an African Farm:*

. . . In truth nothing matters. This dirty little world, full of confusion, and the blue rag, stretched overhead for sky, is so low we could touch it with our hand.

Existence is a great pot, and the old Fate who stirs it round cares nothing what rises to the top and what goes down, and laughs when the bubbles burst. And we do not care. Let it boil about. Why should we trouble ourselves? . . .

A gander drowns itself in our dam. We take it out, and open it on the bank, and kneel looking at it. Above are the organs divided by delicate tissues; below are the intestines artistically curved in a spiral form, and each tier covered by a delicate network of blood-vessels standing out red against the faint blue background. Each branch of the blood-vessels is comprised of a trunk, bifurcating and re-bifurcating into the most delicate hair-like threads, symmetrically arranged. We are struck with its singular beauty, and moreover—and here we drop from our kneeling into a sitting posture—this also we remark: Of that same exact shape and outline is our thorn-tree seen against the sky in mid-winter; of that shape also is delicate metallic tracery between our rocks; in that exact path does our water flow when without a furrow we lead it from the dam; so shaped are the antlers of the horned beetle. How are these things related that such deep union should exist between them all? That would explain it. We nod over the gander's inside.

This thing we call existence—is it not a something which has its roots far down

Panels from the ninth grade History through Drama main lesson

below in the dark, and its branches stretching out into the immensity above, which we among the branches cannot see? Not a chance jumble; a living thing, a *ONE*. The thought gives us intense satisfaction, we cannot tell why.

We nod over the gander; then start up suddenly, look into the blue sky, throw the dead gander and the refuse into the dam, and go to work again.

And so it comes to pass in time that the earth ceases for us to be a weltering chaos. We walk in the great hall of life, looking up and round reverentially. Nothing is despicable—all is meaningful; nothing is small, all is part of the whole, whose beginning and end we know not. The life that throbs in us is a pulsation from it—too mighty for our comprehension, not too small.

And so it comes to pass at last that, whereas the sky was at first a small blue rag stretched over us, and so low that our hands might touch it, pressing down on us, it raises itself into an immeasurable blue arch over our heads, and we begin to live again.

There are a thousand ways, of course, to cultivate the imagination. It goes without saying that each teacher creates his own ways and means. You can steep a boy or a girl in the greatest poems of the greatest poets, read them aloud to him, have him learn them by heart and collect poems as he might collect flowers or autumn leaves, lead him deep into his childhood memories of nature and into his newest experiences of men, minerals, and stars; open him to the sounds, rhythms, and wisdoms of language; show him how with Blake not to "see with but through the eye": how to open eyes within eyes. Let him learn not only to see but to breathe in the color of the sky, the light of a birch, the sunset glow on a snow peak, the gray devastation and tragedy of a city slum. Let this new wind of experience lift him into new flight, to a "new height of view" and wider perspectives from which he may then breathe back not plodding but winged words. This breath stirs more than the mind, it vivifies the whole circulation of a man and strengthens the pulse of the heart. Imagination leads here to inspiration.

The exercises I have suggested earlier are attempts not only to awaken imagination but to help perfect it to as clear and "true" a lens, one as transparent to reality as possible, so that when used creatively it could perhaps become, in Tolstoy's words, a means of dealing "with what man should become." In those exercises we were following, for the most part, in the footsteps of Thoreau, that Yankee pioneer of modern outlook. He, as well as Emerson and Olive Schreiner, took many hints from Goethe and speak in a like spirit. Rudolf Steiner has called attention to the importance of a rediscovery of Goethe as a forerunner of the development of scientific thinking needed in our day. It is through an exact schooling in imagination that Goethe and, to a far greater extent, Steiner himself arrived at insights that point to new advances in science, education, and the arts. And it is this kind of lively but precise and fluid imagination, it would seem, that is going to be necessary in order to do more than bewail the times, and be able to see sense and maintain stability in the changing complexities and impasses that confront us.

We find a recognition of the Goethean ability in Thoreau in an introduction to *Walden* by Sherman Paul in which he writes with imaginative "whole-sight" of the passage quoted earlier:

> The most brilliant passage in "Spring," Thoreau's description of the thaw, was a myth of creation as expression. This elaborate metaphor of the organic process that proceeds from the inside out, that creates and shapes by means of the Idea—the process of Nature, art, moral reform and social reform—was also for Thoreau the metaphor of his purification and rebirth. . . . This evolution from the excremental to aerial forms was a process of purification: . . . "The very globe continually transcends and translates itself, and becomes winged in its orbit." . . .
>
> As he learned from Goethe, the leaf was the unit-form of all creation, the simplest form of which the most complex, even the world, was composed. . . . "The Maker of this earth but patented a leaf." This process, of course, not only applied to art, but to all re-forming and shaping. It illustrated Emerson's belief that "Nature is not fixed but fluid. Spirit alters, moulds, makes it"—that not only poems and individual lives, but institutions were "plastic like clay in the hands of the potter." . . . Thoreau was not the reformer, however, who broke things, but one whose methods, like the thaw with its "gentle persuasion," melted things. . . .
>
> *Walden* is the kind of heroic book that was worthy of "morning discipline," a book so true to "our condition" that reading it might date a new era in our lives.

It is just such a "heroic book," one that does not break but builds, which does in fact appeal to this new generation. Thoreau has never before been so popular. Consciously or unconsciously young people seem to long for this kind of new era, this sort of revolution of vision and action, such a "transcending and translating" of self and social institutions, for which the intellect is a necessary, sharp cutting tool, but which, alone, is powerless to produce.

It is not without significance that the emphasis upon analysis, to which we owe a large portion of the greatness of present civilization, has had its counterpart in racial splits, the splitting of the atom, and even in the split personality. To balance this we may do well, now, to cultivate also analogy, which emphasizes the unifying forces within the variety of races and nations, within the individual and in man's relation to nature.

Imagination makes "Cosmos out of Chaos." In educating it we work not with telescope or microscope but upon the opening, exercising, and polishing of our own lens

Such self-evolution is actually the most revolutionary of acts. It is what we need to help in the reorganization of colleges and high school. We might then give the full responsibility to those who have had experience with young people and understand the similes of their nature, their laws of growth and metamorphoses. The so-called establishment in many cases consists of the dry, paperlike pupa or shell left behind by the human spirit, which longs to build new institutions based upon blueprints of forms more organic to its growing nature. Yet it is these more living, more evolving forms only that fully justify the casting off of the old.

Men schooled in imagination might become teachers, scientists, statesmen, businessmen, artists who are better able to conceive new and more practical creations and solutions, a little abler to see their own ambitions in relation to the whole of society, a little less apt to thrust into the present what will become a danger or pollution in the future.

The healthy awakening and training of imagination may well be one of the most crucial challenges that face educators today.

THE HIGH SCHOOL VISUAL ARTS PROGRAM

Rudolf Steiner School, New York City

Rallou Malliarakis Hamshaw

High school students who live in a big city such as New York are privileged young individuals. One cannot underestimate the extraordinary value that accessible, daily exposure to a vibrant cultural life can play in their lives. These adolescents are encouraged to attend museums and galleries on their own, and not only through field trips with their classes. They have endless opportunities to enjoy a vital, constantly changing art world; this plethora of display makes training students in the visual arts that much more rewarding.

Oil painting by a twelfth grade student

Not too long ago, three of New York's most prestigious museums exhibited the work of two great architects simultaneously: Mies van der Rohe in Berlin at MoMA (Museum of Modern Art), Mies van der Rohe in America at the Whitney, and Frank Gehry at the Guggenheim. What a splendid experience for any interested person to take in all at once. Such exposure is not so easy to come by, but the young New Yorker has it available at his fingertips to seek out, particularly if he is truly interested in art and inclined to broaden his vision.

Whether students are aware of it or not, having easy access to museums, theaters, galleries, happenings, art schools, large environmental sculptures that adorn public places, controversial cultural events such as the "Sensation" exhibit from the Saatchi Collection that was shown at the Brooklyn Museum of Art several years ago—all of these play an important role in contributing to a high school student's cultural education. I see the city as an ally in my endeavor to inspire an appreciation for art and to teach skills. When students at our school go off on a three-week internship program at the end of their senior year, we are often able to place them in professional areas of their choice, including successful galleries, architectural firms, and museums. Such opportunities are just another advantage of city life. E. B. White wrote in his memorable essay "Here is New York":

> New York is the concentrate of art and commerce and sport and religion and entertainment and finance, bringing to the arena the gladiator, the evangelist, the promoter, the actor, the trader and the merchant.
>   New York blends the gift of privacy with the excitement of participation; and better than most dense communities it succeeds in insulating the individual (if he wants it and almost everyone wants or needs it) against all enormous and violent and wonderful events that are happening every minute.

Living in New York City, in spite of its many drawbacks, offers the interested high school student endless opportunities to explore an amazingly diverse art scene and to come into contact with accomplished professionals from all walks of life. It is also helpful for those students who are considering a specialized career in the arts as an option after graduation, to have a choice of art schools in New York City available to them for summer courses, or afternoon and evening classes. Students who attend such schools have a unique opportunity to strengthen their skills and benefit from professional guidance when preparing an appropriate portfolio. Many students that I have taught have done exactly this. Such courses are also available for much younger students who wish to pursue their artwork outside of the Steiner School curriculum.

Maintaining a strong arts program, in which the academic life of the school is balanced by a full exploration of the arts, is also a major draw for parents who are looking for an alternative to traditional education for their children. I do not mean to imply that programs in the arts are unique to Waldorf schools, but they do manage to integrate the arts into the overall curriculum in a more organic and complete manner. At the Rudolf Steiner School in New York, art courses are all mandatory and are not merely offered as electives. This approach immediately takes the experience of "artistic endeavor" off the pedestal, making it an accessible enterprise for every student. Regardless of their natural talent, students achieve a deep sense of satisfaction, and this healthy sense of achievement is reflected in both artistic and academic areas of study, where one discipline enhances the other in a very natural way.

THE ARTS CURRICULUM

Simply being in New York City or any other lively town is certainly no guarantee of a rich experience in art education. How does one actually achieve sophisticated results with fourteen- to eighteen-year-old adolescents—results that are not merely a reflection of the instructor's expertise but a concrete realization of each student's developing artistic personality and individual style? For one thing, the Waldorf curriculum itself helps immeasurably by actively teaching students to appreciate the visual arts, as well as to develop impressive ability and technique at the high school level. The purpose of this curriculum is not to produce professional artists but to inspire the "artistic" in every young person, with the hope of cultivating greater internal sensitivity and soul-life, as well as strengthening the will of creative students.

NINTH-GRADE DRAWING

In Waldorf Schools, we often talk about a curriculum that is age appropriate. For example, it is a meaningful artistic experience for ninth-grade students to work in charcoal and black pastel on large sheets of paper. The medium itself is dramatic and interesting; charcoal is endlessly flexible and possesses genuine aesthetic quality. The growing ninth-grade student with his or her mood swings is by nature a young person of extremes. The strong contrasts of light and shadow, of black, white, and intermediate grays, naturally complement the dramatic emotional personality of the freshman pupil, who is often able to render a picture with considerable power and graphic boldness. In addition to teaching drawing skills, students are encouraged to "observe" form in nature, thus becoming more aware of the world around them. We purposely hold back color at this point and encourage our

Charcoal drawing by a ninth grade student

students to explore the extremes of light and shade through the expressive charcoal medium, free of the challenging and often complicated demands of working with color.

NINTH- AND TENTH-GRADE GRAPHIC ART AND ILLUSTRATION

Designing monograms, book and compact disc jackets, poster designs, and logo and advertisement designs is demanding on an artistic as well as intellectual level. It is also fun and a lively challenge for ninth- and tenth-grade students who are interested in graphic design and illustration. This elective class is new to our high school arts curriculum and one we would like to keep in our program. Students in this class are assigned very specific projects, such as the ones mentioned above, which they need to address in a very clear manner. Type design, for example, requires thought and legibility; an illustration for a book jacket acts as a mini poster and must, at first glance, convey certain essential clues about the story, while a corporate logo design requires a unique union and balance of both type and graphic image. These kinds of exercises help broaden the young designer's intelligence and aid in stimulating his or her imagination. At the end of the course, completely inexperienced students have produced interesting, bold, and often witty designs that strengthen their overall artistic confidence and achievements in very positive ways. Developing a tasteful sense of design can also help students impart greater care in other areas of their schoolwork, such as their main lesson books or other special projects that require artistic judgment.

NINTH- AND TENTH-GRADE BLOCK PRINTING

Linoleum block printing is also offered to ninth- and tenth-grade students as an elective course. Students are taught the fundamentals of block printing with black ink or paint, as well as printing in color. Subject matter varies with each individual student, and participants in the class work at their own pace.

Watercolor painting by a tenth grade student

TENTH-GRADE WATERCOLOR PAINTING

The tenth-grade block in watercolor painting involves the interpretation of a masterwork from art history, namely from movements such as Impressionism, Post-Impressionism, and Fauvism. The purpose of this study is to draw students into the world and private vision of a great artist, where he or she will encounter, through that master's hand, the experience of color. This revolution of color and its enormous impact on the artists of nineteenth-century France gave birth to some of the most exquisite and spontaneous paintings in the whole of art history. This project is a fine way for students to live this color rebellion on quite a deep level while expanding their own competence as young painters.

Watercolor painting by an
eleventh grade student

ELEVENTH-GRADE WATERCOLOR
AND MIXED-MEDIA PAINTING

By eleventh grade, students at a Waldorf school are very able draftsmen and painters. The consistent training of the eye, the act of learning how to see that which began years earlier in elementary school and remained a vital part of the visual arts program in ninth and tenth grades, have now yielded positive and often impressive results. This is clearly seen in the excellent artwork of Waldorf high school students. Eleventh-grade students continue their work in watercolor painting, only on a more sophisticated level. Applying even more subtle nuances of tone and color is demanded of the students. Subject matter varies from year to year. After they have completed a formal studio assignment, students may tackle a free project of their choice. They have the option of using pastel or pencil in conjunction with the watercolor medium, in order to create a mixed-media work. Painting at this level becomes a more personal experience for students. With their skills already intact, they endeavor to push their abilities as far as they can go. The high standards that these art students maintain for themselves, in addition to their growing self-esteem, prepare them beautifully for what comes next: twelfth-grade oil painting.

TWELFTH-GRADE OIL PAINTING

Without the additional reinforcement of watercolor painting in the eleventh grade, students in Waldorf schools would not be as well prepared for the substantial transition from watercolor painting to oil painting as they so often seem to be. The purpose of the eleventh-grade course is to focus even more intently on the students' ability with the medium, thus raising their own expectations for their work. Pursuing their aesthetic sensibilities to a higher level is also a major aim of eleventh-grade painting. There is no question that students who have substantial experience with drawing become better painters. The eighth- and ninth-grade drawing courses at our school successfully help prepare these young artists for their work in painting, which follows in the tenth, eleventh, and twelfth grades.

The oil painting class offered to twelfth-grade students is an elective course in our school. This is a yearlong class that should be taken only by motivated students who wish to learn the basics of oil painting in an intense but supportive studio environment. The transition from watercolor painting to oil painting is quite a natural one. Students work on a project for a much longer period of time. Sustaining interest in a single painting over a number of weeks or even months in certain cases is a major challenge for students and one of the most valuable lessons to be learned from the oil painting class. Participants in this class enjoy the immensely versatile medium of oil paint, with its delightful

Oil painting by a twelfth grade student

plasticity and wide chromatic range. Paint is no longer transparent or translucent; it is opaque and rather dense, which requires an entirely different kind of handling on the part of the students. They begin by applying fairly thin coats of oil paint to establish composition and perspective, gradually building up to a more substantial, tactile surface where the paint becomes thicker. There is no preliminary "sketching out" in pencil first; students paint directly onto the canvas in a loose manner using light coats of color. The senior student eventually confronts himself with a demanding self-portrait, which he or she completes by the end of the course. Apart from reaping its artistic rewards, students who paint with oils learn to control and manipulate the medium to their advantage. They become patient and begin to value good craftsmanship. This experience enriches both the intellectual and cultural life of the students, enabling them to better concentrate on every other aspect of their academic life at school.

FROM REALISM TO SURREALISM: A BRIEF SURVEY OF MODERN EUROPEAN ART, 1840–1930

The Rudolf Steiner School, as we have said, is dedicated to the belief that the practice of the arts enhances a student's life and overall learning experience. It is therefore valuable background material for senior students to study the great modern art movements that originated in Europe, primarily in France, in the mid to late nineteenth century and early twentieth century. These movements produced widespread influence all over the world, culminating, to some degree, in the Armory Show of 1913 in New York City. Here the American public finally worked up to the notion of real "avant-garde" painting, with its abrupt exposure to the Cubist works of Picasso and Braque, to Matisse's color-drenched and liberated canvases from Morocco and the south of France, to samples of Futurism and Russian Constructivism, and to Duchamp's startling "Nude Descending a Staircase." With this stunning exhibition, the art world in America would never be the same.

In a short and intensive main lesson of three or four weeks, senior students trace the beginnings of the modern artist's search for new freedom of expression, beginning with Courbet and the Realist Rebellion and ending with Dali and the Surrealists. Students naturally sympathize with the artist's struggle to find his own unique voice. It is a struggle they can relate to on a very personal level; the many dynamic and often larger-than-life characters they encounter along the way quickly capture their imaginations and inspire their interest in art. Here, New York City once again acts as a partner in making great paintings a reality for students. Taking the senior class to MoMA to see Picasso's "Les Demoiselles d'Avignon," one of the most influential paintings of the twentieth century, is to help them understand the material on a far deeper level than if they had not had the opportunity to see such a compelling work. Certain topics in architecture are also touched upon in this course, such as the Bauhaus movement in Germany and the works of Frank Lloyd Wright in America. In addition to the study of world history, students who are well versed in the history of art are not only better educated young individuals, they are culturally more sensitive and informed. These qualities are part of a truly well rounded Waldorf education at the high school level.

A COMPLEMENTARY AFTERNOON ART BLOCK

This block is scheduled in the afternoons during the run of the history of modern art main lesson. In a composition of their own choosing, students explore a style of painting studied in class, such as Pointillism, Cubism, Realism, or Expressionism. Not unlike the tenth-grade students, who experience their own interpretation of a great masterwork, these senior students solidify their understanding of the art movements they study during the main lesson by actually rendering a picture in the style of painting that has most aroused their interest. One year, students worked from a still-life arrangement and were required to produce an image in the style of Analytical or Synthetic Cubism. This hands-on experience has proven to be a helpful and reinforcing activity for students, one that seems to advance their appreciation of the main lesson material that is delivered every morning, digested over the course of the day, and later reflected in the afternoon art classes in the form of a concrete painting.

STUDIO METHODS AND TECHNIQUES

We have an intelligent curriculum that is fully supportive of the arts; the responsibility of the teacher to inspire and awaken interest must also come into play. Each teacher approaches such a task differently. I would like to describe certain successful methods I have used for many years, and to discuss topics in art teaching that I consider important.

SUBJECT MATTER

Of crucial importance to the success of a project, of course, is choosing the right subject matter for a particular class. How does one decide what project to undertake with a class?

Pastel drawing by a twelfth grade student for the
History through Modern Art main lesson

The choice, in my opinion, is largely intuitive, based primarily on the teacher's knowledge of the class and its needs. The question the art teacher must ask is: "What would be truly valuable subject matter for this particular constellation of students to explore?"

I usually assign a theme that every student in the class addresses at the same time. Working out a "theme" in this way seems to unify the class, creating an interesting energy in the studio. Watching the individuality of each student emerge from common subject matter is always surprising. Every student has his or her unique touch and style, so each completed picture is different, regardless of a consistent theme. The exhibition that results from this approach is often powerful in its visual impact; this has a great deal to do with the consistency of a theme. It is extremely important to exhibit student artwork in as professional a manner as possible, so that students can view their projects objectively and fully appreciate their own achievement and effort.

THE LONG-TERM PROJECT

Hand in hand with casting the appropriate subject matter for a class is the pace and goals of a project. The "long-term" project is a phrase I have used to describe my method of working with high school students at the Rudolf Steiner School. Whether the students are ninth-graders or twelfth-graders, they work on one demanding project over a series of weeks, as opposed to several minor studio assignments. This does not mean that students always produce only one project during an afternoon art block. Some may move on to a free study after completing the main exercise assigned to them; ninth-graders, for example, complete a number of black-and-white studies in drawing class before they tackle a major studio assignment.

Assigning ambitious long-term projects to students has proven to be a valuable tool when teaching painting and drawing on the high school level. A long-term project, by its very nature, is often very difficult, requiring skill, focus, and a deep involvement on the part of the student. Students return to their pictures three times a week, one hour and fifteen minutes each session; as a result, they do not rush their work. Instead, they take their time to analyze the material, thoroughly bringing subtlety and attention to detail to their pictures. They form a special relationship to the work of art they are creating. They also experience the different phases a picture undergoes before it is finally finished: the excitement of the initial beginning, the difficult, stubborn, and often frustrating middle period, and the eventual thrill of the completed piece. The long-term project encourages students to have patience and to maintain high standards of achievement.

SOURCE MATERIAL

In a city like New York, where students have been exposed to the immensely diversified world of the visual arts, the latest achievements by current artists, and cutting-edge exhibitions, it stands to reason that contemporary high school art classes should be broad in their inclusion of modern source material from which students can work. Within reasonable boundaries, of course, any means to a creative end on the part of responsible, enthusiastic, and motivated art students is encouraged. Photographs, for example, provide a rich source of inspiration for students to work from and often serve as a solid point of departure for their work. It is interesting to note that artists such as Degas, Munch, Picasso, and Eakins all used photography (usually their own) as source material for their work.

Unlike the young child who is encouraged to work strictly from his or her imagination, the high school student is in love with realism—the "illusion of reality." He or she is interested in detail and the careful depiction of "things as they appear to be." Observing real life and/or working from photographs (often the student's) or reproductions teaches high school students about form, perspective, and composition. They are encouraged at all times to "interpret," to personalize the material and not copy, to depart from what's in front of their eyes, but to return to the image for guidance when necessary. This balance of imagination and interpretation from a worthy source produces excellent results for the most part. The immediate sense of satisfaction that students derive from their finished, carefully observed projects fuels their commitment to do the very best they can in the art studio and on their own.

WORKING FROM LIFE

It is equally important for students to work from life. Studio still-life arrangements, portraiture and self-portraiture, using each other as models in different poses—these are highly valuable and difficult projects for high school students to undertake. When a beginner works from life, he or she is confronted with the third dimension, the ambiguity of actual, three-dimensional space. It is a hard exercise for such students to "see" the environment in which an object or figure exists. Practice and patience is needed, particularly with ninth-grade students, to achieve real volume in their paintings and drawings. Perceiving depth of space, observing the subtle nuances of color, understanding proportion, particularly as it applies to the figure, are all challenging goals when working from real-life situations in a studio art class.

WHY A FIGURATIVE OR REPRESENTATIONAL APPROACH?

For the most part, I believe it is natural and right to work in a figurative and representational manner with high school students. Picasso and others claimed that in order to abstract nature, one must first know it. The high school student, in my experience, feels gratified when he or she produces a painting or drawing that truly reflects his or her careful observation of the real world. When is it appropriate to allow students to work in an abstract style? There should be no hard-and-fast rule in answer to that question. If there is genuine interest on the part of the student to work in a nonobjective manner, and if she can put abstract form and color from her imagination and render it with commitment, then she is ready to work abstractly. The oil painting elective class, given its steady, run-through structure, is the ideal class for students to attempt abstraction. Oil painting students are seniors and they are more experienced artists at this point. They have also

had the opportunity to study certain modern movements in the twelfth-grade Art History Survey main lesson such as Cubism, Mondrian and De Stijl, and Surrealism.

In my experience, however, most younger high school students are not capable of truly conceptualizing, realizing, and executing an abstract image. And even if they do, the results are not very successful. They tend to be overly playful and even trite at times. These students are either simply too young and visually inexperienced, or, in a totally contradictory sense, they may be too old and too experienced! For example, the first-grader would have no difficulty creating a stunning, nonfigurative picture. Of course, our expectations of students at different ages vary; the first-grader, so involved with mood and color, does not produce an abstract image with a deliberate idea in mind. For him, the experience of painting is largely intuitive.

DEMONSTRATION AS A TEACHING TOOL

When all is said and done, how does one actually teach drawing and painting? Many steps are involved in the process of creating a viable method by which art instructors can attempt to teach interested young people how to paint and draw. In my view, one successful step along the way is to demonstrate to students. No matter how vibrant, articulate, or clear a teacher might be, painting and drawing are visual endeavors; students need to watch and observe in order to understand the basics of how to begin a picture properly. Gustave Courbet, the great French Realist artist, said: "Painting is basically a concrete art, and must concern itself with real and exciting things."

Before every long-term project is started, I very quickly give a brief and loose demonstration to the whole class. If students are painting or drawing landscapes, for example, I may first determine the horizon line in very pale tones or lines, and then sketch out the predominate elements of design in the piece. I do not concentrate on details but work from the whole, leading up to individual parts. I pay particular attention to proportion and the placement of certain key forms on the page. Students will hear me say again and again, "Do the whole thing at the same time!" This is true of portraiture, still-life renderings, landscapes, or even abstract painting. Demonstrating in this way, at the start of a major project, seems to help students (especially very inexperienced students) tackle their ambitious studio assignments with more self-confidence, and a clearer sense of how to begin the marvelous challenge of creating a picture.

Life study by a tenth grade student

Chaos Theory: Description, Not Prediction

Marisha Plotnik

If our education is an art, then the main lesson, in particular, is my canvas and the painting is still in progress. During my eight years at the Rudolf Steiner School, I have introduced new blocks, discarded old ones, and always worked to reshape and reconsider what I am teaching. One project of particular interest to me has been a twelfth-grade block in chaos theory. In many ways, its content is an excellent tool for what I hope to achieve by teaching math and physics in a Waldorf school. One topic it brings into sharp focus is the role of prediction in science and its neglected complement of description.

Science has achieved an unequaled importance in our society, and we take for granted that real science, hard science, is the study of mechanisms. For every possible occurrence, science seeks for the mechanism that caused it and for the laws and equations that govern that mechanism. It is a science of prediction. This ability to predict is essential. Without it, we would drift in an arbitrary world of surprise events, seeing witchcraft everywhere. Prediction has given us advanced technology and the ability to control and manipulate the world to the point of designing our own living organisms. However, there is another side to science, one that is often neglected: this is the science of description. Description is creative. It forces the observer to see the world more carefully, and the larger one's vocabulary for description, the more that emerges to be seen. Prediction narrows one's field of view so that only the expected outcome is seen. Description widens that view to include the anomalous and unexpected outcomes, often windows to radically new ideas about the world.

Chaos theory uses numbers and equations, as does any quantitative science, but it is a science of description, not prediction. This may appear to be a contradiction in terms, but we must admit that for everything that we can predict, there are a far greater number of things we cannot predict. The weather, for example, is notoriously sneaky. We once thought that it was merely because we hadn't enough data, or perhaps hadn't found the right equations. However, it now appears that even if we had every relevant measurement: wind speed, temperature, barometric pressure, and on and on, and we did know all of the equations linking those numbers together, we would still never be able to make accurate predictions very far into the future. This principle of sensitive dependence on initial conditions states that if our initial measurements are imprecise by an arbitrarily small amount—and this they must be, for that is the nature of measurement—then our predictions will be exponentially imprecise, so imprecise as to make them irrelevant. Prediction has come full circle. It was only with the astonishing calculating power of computers, power that allowed us to predict so many things, that we discovered the essential unpredictiveness of chaotic systems.

Mixed media drawing by an eleventh grade student

Where chaos theory on one side sets a limit to our powers of prediction, it opens up to us on the other side an expanded power to describe. Chaos theory describes the complex and intricate forms of nature in their own language. The Euclidean geometry of circles, squares, and triangles is woefully inadequate when it comes to describing a tree, but chaos has a new geometry, fractal geometry, that mathematically describes nature's forms. Fractal dimension, unlike the familiar Euclidean dimensions of zero, one, two, and three, is never a whole number. A dimension of 1.6 is a perfect description for a line that is almost a surface, a line that twists and turns and snakes back upon itself so many times that it almost becomes a surface, a line that has a gigantic length but confines a small, finite area, like the rocky, inlet-rich coastline of Great Britain.

These fractals not only describe the forms of nature, they also arise from plotting on a graph the results of repeating a calculation again and again. However, this is not the kind of graphing every high school student knows well, where given an equation an x is chosen and plugged in, the y is found, and one point is plotted on the page. Rather, this is a graphing of the nature of those equations. By iterating the function over and over, will the numbers settle down or will they spiral out of control? This kind of graphing, a graphing that takes into account time as well as space, yields that strange, buglike Mandelbrot set, where zooming in on a tiny section reveals Dr. Seuss forms and then, hidden within them, more bugs. These images are self-similar: each part is an image of the whole, as the branch is an image of the tree and the tributary an image of the whole river. Something of nature is again described.

I am often asked what "use" there is to chaos theory. This question only arises if we see prediction as the purpose of science. I argue that there is equal value in description. By describing appropriately we see, then recognize, a part of the world we had never noticed before. We weave connections and make our experience whole. Understanding a phenomenon does not mean identifying a mechanism; rather, it is this process of making connections to the rest of our experience. The more connections we make, the more meaningful the world becomes. It is this kind of understanding that I see as the purpose of science, and provoking my students to make connections is what I strive to do as a teacher.

Communications Technology in the Waldorf High School

Richard Oliver

The very soul of education is human communication. One of the most active and controversial areas of curriculum development today in Waldorf schools—as well as most others—is the expanding role of communications technology. By "communications technology" I mean devices that human beings have created to record, process, transmit, and reproduce words, symbols, sounds, and/or visual images.

It may be a worthy goal to help students feel at home in a world dominated by information machines, or to give them a basic level of practice and comfort with computer hardware and software by the time they graduate. Yet in a Waldorf school, we aim to look much deeper into the role of technology in human development and in society. Our curriculum must consider the effects, both positive and negative, that the presence of computer technology may have on:

- the social life of students and atmosphere of the school

- the aesthetic and inspirational quality of the educational experience

- the depth and clarity of students' thinking and academic work

- the warmth and compassion with which students meet the world

- the power of students to work hard toward their highest ideals

- the flexibility and creativity that students bring to art and to life

Communications technology has the potential to strongly influence all of these, and this potential—both constructive and destructive—will only grow in the future. Each young person meeting these technologies is confronted with the potential to think and act with almost unimaginable clarity, precision, complexity, and creative power. They are also confronted with an equal potential for addictive, dispassionate destruction. As educators, we must clearly tread with extraordinary caution as we prepare a place for this meeting.

Our challenges may include helping students to:

- develop the ability to think in discrete, logical steps when appropriate while also fostering more fluid, creative forms of thought;

- learn to create "virtual realities" to be experienced by others—both written words and audiovisual recordings—while remaining fully aware of the deep responsibility for another's soul that this entails;

- discover the freedom of expression that digital technologies can provide without becoming addicted to and unable to express one's self without them;

- fully understand the scientific/technological worldview out of which so much of our society and surroundings have been created, while remaining free to question its most fundamental tenets.

Because the capacity for this level of reasoning and responsibility only truly develops during the high school years, Waldorf schools seldom introduce communications technology before the ninth grade. Each school and teacher must find its own unique approach, yet three essential aspects of a communications technology curriculum are found in some form in nearly all Waldorf high schools today:

INTEGRATION OF APPROPRIATE COMPUTER USE IN HUMANITIES, MATH, AND SCIENCE CLASSES

We don't teach courses in "paintbrushes," "paper and pencil," or "microscope." Instead, we teach courses in the arts, humanities, and sciences. The techniques for using tools are introduced as necessary and appropriate, but always in the context of higher human purposes that the tools help us strive toward. Like a library, a campus communications network is not a separate subject area but rather a "master tool" that every teacher and student may turn to during their study.

In the social studies and health curriculum, students examine the effects of communications technology use on society and the individual in our times. In English, math, and science, use of word processors and spreadsheets may be gradually brought in as students reach a level of facility with words and numbers that warrants a stronger emphasis on editing multiple drafts. As students near adulthood, modern topics such as chaos theory and research skills will naturally prompt discussion and use of communications technology.

COMMUNICATIONS TECHNOLOGY
MAIN LESSON BLOCKS

Typically, ninth- and/or tenth-grade blocks introduce the fundamental principles of message encoding, transmission, and storage. The emphasis at this age level is on exploring and understanding human communication itself, and hands-on work constructing circuits that allow the transmission and storage of meaningful messages from one heart and mind to another.

Eleventh- and/or twelfth-grade blocks cover information theory, software and database design, and mathematical logic. If these blocks are taught with a strong biographical and historical emphasis, they can help unify the many fields of mathematics studied throughout high school as well as offer an intimate view of modern history and its relationship to math and science.

A "DIGITAL ARTS" STUDIO WHERE STUDENTS
LEARN ARTISTIC APPLICATIONS OF COMPUTERS

If we wish to truly integrate communications technology into our curriculum, the most powerful and effective way to do so is through the arts. An increasing number of Waldorf high schools introduce students to modern graphics design, typography, digital photography, sound recording and production, cinematography, 3D computer modeling, and interactive arts.

Each of these art forms has the potential, if taught in a developmentally appropriate way, to provide a "crown jewel" to the students' study of traditional visual and performance arts. In each case, the role of technology is to empower the artist to "step outside" the art form and become an "editor" of the artwork or performance in the same way that the creative writer must learn to not only write well but also rewrite with the reader's experience in mind.

In essence, all three aspects of this curriculum address the same central question: Can young people today be introduced to technology in such a way that they master it, rather than it mastering them? My own approach when carrying this question into the classroom is to follow several principles that extend throughout Waldorf education:

- avoid using a technology in the classroom until students truly understand the principles behind its operation and construction;

- develop an understanding of technology by designing and building it, and by learning about the thoughts of the individuals who invented it;

- protect students from technologies that cannot be mastered without inner capacities they haven't yet developed;

- provide only educational experiences that answer a "calling" within the students at their current stage of development.

Finding the appropriate role for communications technology is therefore not a simple matter of deciding when to offer a "computers" class, or deciding where to put a "computer room." As adults, our biggest planning challenge may be to avoid thinking in terms of an outdated idea of large, expensive stationary "computers" arranged in neat rows and housed in a room of their own. A more realistic analogy would be to think of a new kind of paper—that is, paper that can record and convey information in a much more flexible, animated, multisensory fashion.

Instead of asking ourselves where to put information-processing machines in our schools, we instead face the reality that they are becoming as ubiquitous as notebooks and pencils and will be everywhere that we do not expressly prohibit them. Given the rate at which our society is moving toward a "totally connected" world permeated with instant communications, it is no small task to anticipate and guide how this transforms our schools and students.

Should schools "just say no" to the great "electronic drug," or should we encourage technology use and "bring Waldorf education into the twenty-first century"? Our charge as educators today is to navigate carefully between these extremes, embracing communications technology only where it is truly essential in awakening human capacities for clear thought, deep compassion, and strong will.

MORALITY AND THE TEACHING OF LITERATURE IN THE HIGH SCHOOL

Carol Bärtges

The word "morality" is once again in vogue in educational circles. With the images of Columbine High School still alive in our collective consciousness, teachers and parents are asking how schools can instill a sense of purpose and humanity in young people. And yet, morality is a loaded term—a word as likely to be associated with sullen pedantry or inflexible demand as it is with good teaching. Modern educators, it seems, are convinced that an ethical education is not the province of the English or biology class but belongs in separate seminars on "anger modifications," racial tolerance," or "community awareness."

To the Waldorf educator, moral education belongs in the classroom. It involves the attempt to help students understand truths beyond their personal parameters, truths that lift them above their narrow concerns and allow them to regard the struggles and quests of mankind with empathy and discernment. As George Eliot observed in her novel *Middlemarch*, "We are all of us born in moral stupidity, taking the world as an udder to feed our supreme selves." Eliot's aim is not to rub our human deficiencies in our all-too-human faces, but rather to emphasize that only when we overcome our self-preoccupation and prejudices can we accomplish anything of note for the world. True judgment is an acquired trait, cultivated consciously and slowly, and in some cases painfully, as was the case for the novel's Dorothea Brooke.

In the English class, the study of great writers and their works is one way of helping the students assume a balanced moral stance, outgrow their "moral stupidity," and develop critical faculties that result in a lawful, compassionate view of the world. Only this kind of judgment can resolve the social fragmentation and isolation young people experience today.

We high school teachers are helped by the work that has been done in the lower grades. My colleague Sandra Williams, who taught at the Kimberton Waldorf School, once said of students with a Waldorf background, "Their appreciation and sense for the great ages of mankind is a brilliant tapestry gleaming with images of heroes and saints, with memories of deeds of honor, valor, and nobility. All these have been impressed upon the soul in a grand tableau transcending time and space."

The experience that students will have in a Waldorf high school is not predicated upon their having attended a Waldorf lower school, but students who arrive with those first eight years of Waldorf schooling do bring a reservoir of powerful images on which they can continually draw to enliven their intellect. Iconoclasts in the best sense of the word, Waldorf students turn out to be more comfortable in thinking "outside the box" than in conforming to safe expectations. Building upon what has been given by an extraordinary school curriculum affirms the students' longing for the ideal in the contemporary world by consciously schooling, developing, and, ultimately, liberating their powers of thought. In their next four years, students learn that freedom in thinking can lead to purposeful moral deeds in the world.

The development of analytical thinking is cultivated in deliberate fashion in a Waldorf English class. Although freshmen and sophomores demonstrate daily that they are more than capable of passing judgment (as they do readily about parents, teachers, and others), a peek into their classrooms quickly shows that young adolescents are not, at this stage, objective. Events are still viewed mostly through the prisms of their emerging individualities. Discussing a book or poem with ninth-graders from a purely abstract, intellectual point of view results in either a volley of personal opinion or an exchange of banalities. Caught in the pendulum of mood swings that propel them to and fro between despair and exhilaration, ninth- and tenth-graders are still striving for equilibrium.

Rudolf Steiner described students of this age as needing to look out into the world of experience and to ground themselves in their surroundings. Therefore, the approach to literature is most effective for this age group when it remains concrete, when it can direct the students toward objective observation. In their reflecting upon and comparing known realities, presented by the teacher and the curriculum, a reconciliation of extremes is brought about that is healing to the mind and to the soul. One might compare Egyptian civilization to the Greek, the Athenian world of law to the fairy world of the woods (*A Midsummer Night's Dream*), the nobility of Odysseus to the power of Menelaus (the *Odyssey*), vowel sounds to consonant sounds, or the internal monologue of Dorothy Parker's "The Waltz" to Ring Lardner's monologue in "Haircut."

Literary conclusions reached in this way, through analogy, the comparison of unlike things, are deeply satisfying and real to ninth- and tenth-graders. They are less apt to make snap judgments when they have lived deeply in two conflicting points of view, for they intuitively find the fulcrum and learn to understand, not condemn, differences.

By regarding the schooling of thought as a slow, evolving process, the Waldorf English teacher helps the students build a sturdy structure in which they will house their slowly developing powers of perception. By senior year, students complete the golden turrets and spires themselves. They have grown adept at making literary connections and analogies of their own. In this way one can honestly describe the experience of the high school English classes as the movement from observation (ninth grade) to insight (twelfth grade).

Not only the teaching approach but also the actual content of the English curriculum itself brings about emotional equilibrium and genuine moral thought. The careful design of the various main lessons throughout the four years allows us to teach what T. S. Eliot calls the "objective correlatives" of literature, those images that will reverberate most deeply in the soul of the student at his or her particular age. If one studies what Rudolf Steiner asserts about the inner life of a fifteen-year-old, for example, one understands the all-important role that community plays in a student's life at this time. Epic literature, with its depiction of Beowulf or Odysseus as representatives of *aristos* (noble society) engaged in *aristae* (noble deeds), strikes a note in the tenth-grader who yearns to conform to a worthy community. The discussion of what constitutes a worthy society addresses this deep and unconscious question for the sophomore. The sixteen-year-old who is more withdrawn takes an inner journey, questing for identity and love while questioning conventions of society. Juniors respond deeply to the archetypes of these experiences presented in eleventh-grade main lessons on *Hamlet, Parzival,* or Romantic poetry. Although a ninth-grader could certainly appreciate the prince of Denmark, the sixteen-year-old's gestalt connects him or her actively to Hamlet's feelings of disenchantment, to the inner struggles of that "profound heart."

Finally, one experiences time and time again that amazing turn in the twelfth grade when the students lift themselves out of subjective contemplation and demonstrate a craving for contact with the world of ideas. Now they are ripe for discussions about literary genres, political movements, and the socioeconomic ramifications of scientific research. What powers of thought the seniors bring to such courses as Transcendentalism or Russian Literature, where they are asked to wrestle with the very act of thinking itself and recognize its moral implications in the world of action! In these twelfth-grade courses, as students discuss Nihilism, Orthodoxy, passive resistance, social reform, or Emerson's concept of beauty and the oversoul, they realize that free thought is often the hallmark of moral deeds. Individuals such as Thoreau, Tolstoy, and Gandhi endeavored to conduct their lives and make choices on the basis of truth alone.

In its conveyance of truth and beauty, in nature and mankind, good literature is always, irrefutably, oral. This is why Alexander Solzhenitsyn, in his 1972 Nobel Prize acceptance speech, said the following:

Who will help us coordinate our scale of values?
What will give mankind one single way of reading its
instruments both for wrongdoing and doing good,
for the intolerable and the tolerable? Who will make
clear for mankind what is really oppressive and unbearable
and what, for being so near, rubs us the
wrong way? Who is capable of extending his understanding
across the boundaries of his own personal
experience? Who has the skill to make a narrow,
obstinate human being aware of others' far-off grief
and joy, to make him understand dimensions and
delusions he himself has never lived through? Propaganda,
coercion, and scientific proofs are all powerless.
But happily, in our world there is a way. It is
art and it is literature.

Out of an understanding of Rudolf Steiner's picture of the inner development of the adolescent, English teachers in a Waldorf high school attempt to bring to the students images in literature that organically cultivate objective, moral thought. In this way, we can help young people learn to transcend their own limitations, approach their fellow human beings with compassion, and actively unite themselves with an ever-changing world.

THE ART OF THINKING*
Helping Students Develop Their Faculties of Thinking and Observation

Craig Holdrege

1

In this two-part essay I examine different facets of thinking we want to help high school students develop. As a science teacher, I give examples out of my own lessons. I want to illustrate how the way we present the subject matter can help awaken and strengthen the students' ability to fathom the world and themselves.

QUESTIONING

The ability to question lies at the root of thinking. When we truly think—and don't just mimic what another person tells us—the activity arises out of questions. Questions are the driving force of any thought process; they give direction, focus, and energy. If we're interested in helping students think, then we must help them learn to question themselves and the world.

One problem with our information age is that people "know" very much without ever having asked for this knowledge or, afterward, questioning it. We know the earth moves around the sun, we know the earth is 4.5 billion years old, we know we breathe oxygen, we know genes determine heredity—we know, we know, we know. But ask ninth-graders *how* they know any of these facts and you get blank stares and responses like "I don't know, somebody told me that," or "I saw it on the Discovery Channel."

The purpose of this question is not to embarrass students but to show them that most of us have no idea how we know what we know. In fact, we are believers in the "facts" of science. It's paradoxical that the scientific age, which began as a revolt against traditional belief systems, has become an age of the belief in science. We are ensconced in a "dogmatic slumber,"

* This essay appeared in two parts in *Renewal* (Fall–Winter 2001 and Spring–Summer 2002).

to use Kant's phrase. One primary task of science teaching should be to help students awaken from a certain naïveté of childhood that can all too easily become a very firm dogmatic slumber in adulthood. Adolescents should feel continual scientific revolution.

To this aim, when I teach science classes beginning in the ninth grade, I emphasize that the students shouldn't take any handed-down knowledge for granted; we need to question what we think we know. In this sense high school students need to become healthy skeptics (not cynics!). "How do I know this?" is the fundamental question. When we begin questioning in this way, we soon realize that we know very little. Although at first unsettling, this realization becomes exhilarating. And there is a person who can stand as an ideal for the students—Socrates, one of the great figures of Western culture who was put to death for thinking independently. He was the man who always asked questions and was wise because he knew that he knew nothing. Starting from this Socratic base, we can begin to build more knowledge.

But this is difficult. If you think back on your experience of science classes in college, high school, or middle school, you may well remember, as I do, learning (and forgetting) myriad facts for multiple-choice tests. This kind of learning is widespread in American education and is what my colleague Steve Talbott calls "fact-shoveling." Since most of us have grown up in this system, it's not easy to overcome the idea that the science teacher's main task is to teach loads of facts. And even worse is the reasoning that we must do this in high school to prepare for college. (Nothing like eating an appetizer of rocks to prepare for the main course of boulders.) So how do we overcome such a dead approach to science?

RIDDLES—THE "SERAPIS TEMPLE"

One powerful and fruitful way to avoid feeding students stones is to present scientific phenomena through concrete examples that are riddles. Riddles engage the mind and stimulate questions. Riddles stir feelings, awakening wonder and interest. Riddles fire the will to find a solution. Riddles are wonderful. The most time-consuming part of preparation for my lessons has been in search of good riddles to serve as the entryway into the process of learning science.

Let's take an example out of the ninth-grade geology block. Rocks don't naturally interest everyone, and the first time I taught the block I was scared to death that I was going to bore the students to death with things I was very excited about. But the riddle approach (along with fieldwork, which I won't go into here) saved the day.

In the eighteenth century Italians began to excavate ruins from the Roman Empire. In Pozzuoli, a village on the Mediterranean coast near Naples, the ruins of what appeared to be a temple were discovered. The tops of three large columns were found hidden by bushes, about a hundred feet from the sea. The columns were covered with foot after foot of compacted volcanic ash (tuff), volcanic rocks (pumice), and debris. Volcanoes surround the area and Vesuvius is not far away; it is an area with frequent earthquakes. The three columns turned out to be enormous—about forty-two feet high. Remains of many other columns were found and the ruins were given the name Serapis Temple. (Later, archaeologists concluded that it was a marketplace.)

There was something strange about the columns (see figure). The lower twelve feet were smooth and uninjured, but the following twelve feet were not: the limestone was highly corroded. Looking carefully, the excavators found cavities with shells of saltwater mussels. These are mussels that bore cavities into rock by dissolving it and then dwell in these cavities. The upper eighteen feet of the columns were weathered but in quite good shape.

If I've succeeded in describing this discovery to the students in a vivid manner, I hardly even need to ask the question, What's going on here? It's as if the columns themselves were saying, Do you see that we are a riddle to be solved? The main question revolves around the twelve-foot band in the middle of the columns that is corroded and full of mussel shells. To the logical minds of ninth-graders it is completely clear that the presence of mussel shells means that the columns were at some point in water. And they must have been in water for quite a long while, since the mussels had time to eat limestone away.

The Serapis Temple columns

Here a process of question and answer begins, where the teacher may need to fill in more information to give the students a better orientation. But the students' conjectures and questions move the process along, which is a bit different in every class.

How did the columns get in water and why is there only one band of corroded limestone, with intact material above and below it? Most students think (as did the first geologists investigating this example) that the water level rose. If this were true, then sea level must have risen at least twenty-four feet, up to the top of the mussel-eaten band in the columns. Since the sea level is more or less horizontal and the Mediterranean Sea is connected to the Atlantic Ocean, the whole oceanic body of water covering the earth would have to have risen—perhaps due to melting of the ice caps—twenty-four feet. This would've resulted in a continuous band of submerged coastlines all over the earth. But this is not the case. Even along the Mediterranean Sea coast there is no evidence for a general rise in sea level. Evidently it was a more local phenomenon.

So what is the alternative? The earth itself could have sunk. Usually someone conjectures that during one or more earthquakes the coast at Pozzuoli sank. The water level appeared to rise, but in reality the earth's surface sank at least twenty-four feet over a period of time. Although this is hard to picture, what else could have happened?

Now we have the columns standing in twenty-four feet of water. Why don't the mussels eat away the whole submerged part of the columns? This is a key moment for thinking—the ability to bring together different facts and see connections. I've seen students' faces light up when they "get it": after or while sinking, a volcano erupts and covers the area with twelve feet of volcanic ash and rock. This protects the lower twelve feet of the columns, so the boring mussels have only the middle twelve feet to inhabit. The upper eighteen feet are above the waterline; they weather but are inaccessible to the water-bound mussels. Slowly the mussels inhabited the twelve-foot band of the columns and ate away limestone, making caves for themselves.

At some point in time the coast must have risen, the water receded, and the columns then stood, once again, on dry ground. Over time they were covered by ash and rock from other volcanoes and debris from earthquakes, so only the tops were visible in the eighteenth century when they were excavated.

Together we have reconstructed in our minds—on hand of three "lowly" columns —remarkable movements of the earth's crust: first sinking, then lifting; and all this within historical times. At the conclusion of this discussion I feel a sense of success when I see that the students are amazed at both what the earth does as well as at their own ability to think and tie together archaeological and geological facts into a cohesive picture.

LOGICAL THINKING ANCHORED IN OBSERVATION

How have the students trained their thinking by learning about the Serapis Temple? First, they have learned that questions are essential. Without asking questions they won't get anywhere. Second, they learn that to answer questions you have to go through a process that takes time and energy. They can't sit back and become enlightened. When they come up with conjectures, then these conjectures have to be brought in relation to the facts at hand. Do they fit? They have to think through consequences: if the sea level rises twenty-four feet, then what would happen on all coastlines? They then see that a particular train of thought doesn't make sense and try a different pathway.

Often, students who are very quick intellectually are also satisfied with answers that don't hold up under further scrutiny. Considering an example like the Serapis Temple columns slows down and extends the thought process so that it can become more conscious. We move from one phenomenon to the next, testing our thoughts at every step. Sometimes we rush ahead only to realize we've lost the phenomena; so we go back and reconsider. Thinking learns to be disciplined, and a core element in this discipline is learning that we need to observe very carefully and be faithful to these observations. Any training of thinking is a training of observation as well (and vice versa).

In adolescence it's very important for students to experience that they can solve riddles. That their questions can be answered. This gives them the confidence they need to feel in their mental powers: I can understand the world. This is not the same thing as the ability to make quick and cutting judgments, a capacity that comes as a kind of adolescent birthright. I have often felt that there is no way to compete with the sharpness of a ninth- or tenth-grader's intellect, which comes out most strongly in the ability to argue. But this capacity to argue and judge often wells from a raging current of moods, likes, and dislikes that can cover up the real idealism they bring into the world. So what the students need to learn—and that is an essential task in the high school—is to base their judgments on interactions with the world and not just on their own predilections. This is why studying the external world in science classes is so healthy.

Through teaching examples of scientific discovery, the students also learn to see science as a product of human activity. Science always starts with riddles like the three columns. Taken in a purely external way, the columns are just things we could pass by and shrug our shoulders at ("so what"). But if we look and question, this static outer appearance transforms in thought into a lively movement. The students begin to see through the columns a world of becoming. They look, so to speak, with their mind's eye into the past by reading the present carefully and intensely. This is vastly different from learning in a geology class the "fact" that the earth's crust moves up and down, illustrated by a few cursory examples. Such "knowledge" remains external to the human soul and is one reason many people learn to dislike science in school. But if the students themselves reconstruct out of the present the past, then they are involved. They know how geological knowledge about the earth's past comes about because they were engaged in a process.

This is a very satisfying experience. And part of that experience is knowing that they don't know all the answers. There is always more to investigate. This experience is the entryway into complex and, then, holistic thinking, which I will discuss in the second part of this essay.

2

In part 1 of this essay I discussed some basic elements of thinking that we can work with in a focused way in the ninth and tenth grades. We want to awaken questions and the students' interest by showing how the world continually presents us with riddles. Answering such riddles is a process and takes work. It means learning to think logically and continually returning to the facts to correct ourselves. Gaining this kind of discipline allows us to proceed further with the students. We see how we need to achieve even greater capacities of thought to do justice to the phenomena of the world. That is the theme of part 2 of this essay.

COMPLEX THINKING: THE GERM THEORY OF DISEASE

As thinkers we have a tendency to simplify matters. Just because a train of thought is logical and clear does not mean it does justice to the phenomena. In fact, when the succession of thoughts becomes exceedingly precise and consistent in itself, we can be quite sure that we're losing sight of the richness of the phenomena we're trying to illuminate. Especially in the ninth and tenth grades, when students should gain confidence and discipline in their thinking abilities, we can live with a certain degree of oversimplification, since we're training "thought muscles." But in the eleventh and twelfth grades we can begin to challenge the students more.

By taking different points of view to consider any given phenomenon or problem, students learn that the world is complex and that we need to adapt ourselves to this complexity. Otherwise we'll end up with schematic notions, or, even worse, caricatures of reality. I believe Rudolf Steiner had this task in mind when, in speaking about the biology curriculum in the eleventh grade, he said that the teacher should emphasize mutual dependency, or reciprocal causation (*Wechselursachenverhältnis*) and go beyond what we call today linear causality (said at a meeting with teachers, June 21, 1922).

I'd like to illustrate complex thinking by considering the germ theory of disease, which I often discuss in an eleventh-grade biology block. This is an especially good topic because it not only challenges the students' mind and opinions but also gives them a picture of how science actually develops. Again, I avoid a general discussion of the topic and use instead historical examples that can capture the students' interest.

Cholera is a deadly disease that spreads in epidemics. People who become ill with cholera suffer severe diarrhea and vomiting. Losing such large quantities of bodily fluids over a short period of time—hours to a couple of days—leads to dehydration and, if nothing changes, death. Nineteenth-century Europe witnessed numerous cholera epidemics. In 1854 a cholera epidemic befell the city and environs of Munich, Germany. Max von Pettenkofer, a medical doctor and professor at the University of Munich, was asked to investigate the epidemic. He began by making a precise map of the outbreak. He found that parts of the city were being ravaged while others were spared. Areas near or along creeks, rivers, and canals as well as low-lying areas near water were especially hard hit. On hills and near watersheds the incidence of cholera was much lower. He also discovered that where the soil was porous there was more cholera than in areas with poor drainage, where the water ran away more on the surface rather than seeping into the ground.

Pettenkofer noticed that the cholera areas were often poor and filthy. The air was filled with the horrible stench from open sewage pits and outhouses. "How gross!" say the students. They don't realize that American and European cities only began to have central sewage systems beginning in the late nineteenth century. The sewage pits were usually not sealed and the contents seeped into the soil. Wells were often contaminated with sewage. Pettenkofer was soon convinced that the interplay of excrement and water was a major factor in the cholera epidemic.

He didn't believe, however, that cholera was simply being passed from one person to the next. He observed many cases in which only some members of a family became ill, and doctors and other caregivers, who regularly came into bodily contact with ill people, usually did not become ill. Evidently, each person has a physiological disposition or constitution that makes him or her more or less susceptible to the disease. Pettenkofer concluded that the proximity to water, unsanitary conditions, and poor health conditions were together responsible for cholera. He worked hard to change these conditions and is often considered one of the fathers of public health and hygiene. Through his efforts Munich became one of the first cities to install centralized sewage and water systems. Everywhere where sanitation increased, cholera ceased to be a problem.

Another German medical doctor and scientist, Robert Koch, was also working to find what caused cholera. Koch traveled to Egypt and India to investigate outbreaks of cholera in the early 1880s. He performed autopsies on the bodies of people who had died of cholera. In every case, he discovered comma-shaped bacteria in the intestinal walls. He never found these bacteria in healthy people. Since intestinal dysfunction brings about the severe diarrhea in cholera, couldn't these bacteria be causing the disease? Is Koch's discovery a proof of the germ theory of disease? Since all the students "know" (recall the problem I described at the beginning of part 1 of this article) that "germs" (bacteria and viruses) cause disease, most students think, "Yes." But with prodding, the students can recognize there is a still a question. That Koch found the bacteria in the corpses doesn't mean they caused the disease. Not only that, I've had students say, the bacteria might be an *effect* of the disease: because people are sick, bacteria can thrive in them. We don't really know—and Robert Koch didn't either.

Koch was an extremely careful and conscientious scientist. He was not prone to making overblown claims and wanted facts to be his judge. So he took infected tissue and learned how to grow the bacteria in laboratory cultures. (This was a momentous step forward in the history of bacteriology; most techniques for growing bacteria were discovered and perfected by Koch and his assistants.) Koch then injected animals—mice, rats, guinea pigs, rabbits—with the bacteria. They usually died of cholera-like symptoms. He isolated the bacteria from the intestines of the dead animals, cultured them, and injected other animals, who also died. He repeated this process of isolation, culturing, and injecting again and again.* To his mind, Koch showed in this way that the comma-shaped bacteria were clearly causing cholera. This was 1883.

Koch had observed in India that people were drinking from the same water in which they bathed, washed clothes, and children defecated. He concluded that the bacteria—which are excreted in large amounts in the diarrhea of the sick—are spread from person to person, which is what causes an epidemic.

Pettenkofer, while not denying the existence of the bacteria, did not believe that they were the sole cause of the cholera. He was so convinced of his opinion—which was based on years of work and experience—that he decided to do an experiment on himself. He would drink a culture of the bacteria to bring to an end what he considered to be an

---

* Some students are rightfully appalled by the description of animal experiments that cause suffering and death in many animals. Often, a lively discussion ensues concerning the pros and cons of animal experimentation in medicine and about the question of animal rights. In this way a historical example brings us into a discussion of important contemporary issues.

irrational fear of bacteria. He had a fresh culture of cholera bacteria sent to him. It contained about a billion bacteria. Before ingesting it, he drank bicarbonate solution to neutralize the acid in the stomach that normally kills bacteria—he didn't want any critics saying afterward that he hadn't done a thorough experiment.

So Pettenkofer drank a culture of cholera bacteria. The next day he awoke and felt fine and was happy to speak with reporters at his home—who had expected to find him dead. Three days later he had strong diarrhea, but it soon subsided and he never fell ill. (Soon thereafter one of his assistants repeated the experiment with similar results, except that he became feverish.)

A lively classroom discussion usually follows this description. "Wasn't Pettenkofer stupid?" "But he survived!" "He was just lucky!" When things have calmed down, we can begin to sort out the situation. What did Pettenkofer prove? He showed that the cholera bacteria are not the sole cause of cholera; if they were, he would have died. Did he prove that the bacteria have nothing to do with cholera? No. Rather, his experiment was a proof of his idea that the individual constitution is a very important factor in contracting the disease. It seems that both Koch and Pettenkofer were partially right and partially wrong. Together, the facts they pointed to provided a correct picture of infectious diseases: they are transmitted by the bacteria (or viruses), but whether the person becomes ill or not is dependent on his or her susceptibility. Only the interplay of these two factors—germ and constitution—mediated by the environment gives rise to an infectious disease.

I go on to discuss with the students that we must be very careful when using the word *cause* in biology. I present other examples, sometimes quoting excerpts from scientific articles that use the word cause. The students are now more critical and wakeful listeners and usually see for themselves that what is called a cause is usually only a partial cause.

Closer investigation always shows that biological phenomena are caused by the interaction of multiple factors. For this reason, I give the students a radical suggestion: to ban the word *cause* from biological and medical vocabulary. Its imprecise usage fosters a great deal of unclarity. We would do well to substitute the word *condition* for the word *cause*. We can say that bacteria present a necessary condition for the outbreak of cholera, but alone they are not sufficient to do so. A weak constitution is also a necessary condition. All the necessary conditions taken together can be said to cause the disease. When the students have understood this, they have entered the school of complex thinking. They see that we need more refined concepts to grasp the world adequately.

Complex thinking is not satisfied with simple answers. It always seeks to find the boundaries of theories and explanations in order to delve deeper into the matter. In the best sense of the word, complex thinking is critical. But it is also comprehensive and flexible in the continual search for new vantage points from which to illuminate a problem.

There are many courses in the eleventh and twelfth grades that are especially well suited to cultivate complex thinking (which doesn't mean it can't be practiced in every subject). I think, for example, of the history of atomism in eleventh-grade chemistry, where students can learn about the evolution of atomic models and overcome the billiard ball pictures they carry in their minds. Or the projective geometry block, where the students confront concepts like infinity and duality (polarity) that stretch their minds in a wonderful way. At Hawthorne Valley School we instituted an ecology block in the eleventh grade. Ecology is *the* scientific discipline that should (but unfortunately often doesn't) make complex thinking fundamental to its teaching, since ecology has everywhere to do with complex, changing relations. Most ecological problems are the stark testament of our inability to think complexly—or one could also say ecologically.

HOLISTIC THINKING

The flexibility of thought we exercise in complex thinking is a prerequisite to understand living phenomena. But it is not enough. I sometimes begin the twelfth grade zoology block by showing the students a picture of an animal they know, say, a cow, and then ask them how they would scientifically explain a cow. The question catches them a bit off guard. But someone usually comes up with a comment such as "The cow has horns to protect itself." Once this kind of answer has fallen, a cascade follows. The cow has a tail to kill insects, it has wide-set eyes to see its prey, it has big molars to grind grass, it has hooves to stand for long periods of time, it has a four-chambered stomach to digest grass. And so on. We go through many characteristics and explain each one by finding some function it fulfills. This kind of explanation is relatively satisfying. Whether they know it or not, the students have applied a popular form of Darwinian thought to the cow. I tell them how in Darwinian theory today researchers look at the different traits of an organism and consider them to be survival strategies. The "reason to be" for any given characteristic is that it allowed the cow to survive. On this theory, each characteristic arises separately and by chance, but because it is supportive of the animal's survival and its ability to reproduce, it is maintained in evolution.

When we've painted this picture, I ask the students to look at what the cow has become conceptually for them. The answer is: an agglomeration of separate characteristics. The cow as a cohering, whole organism that *has* these characteristics has disappeared. But don't we want to understand the cow? The students can see a dilemma. We need to analyze in order to come to any kind of understanding, otherwise we remain in dreamy generalities. But if we lose the whole animal in this process, then what have we gained?

The question is, can we learn to move beyond analysis and discover how the seemingly separate parts of an organism are in fact related to each other within the context of the whole creature? This is the underlying task of the twelfth-grade zoology block.

It's an intriguing fact that while Darwinism has led to an increasingly atomized view of organisms, Charles Darwin himself was keenly aware of the "exquisite adaptation of one part of the organization to another part" (*The Origin of Species*, ch. 3, p. 114). The wings of a bird are of course wonderfully adapted to flight. But the capacity to fly is also expressed in its bone and muscle structures, in its lungs and circulatory system, in its senses and nerves; in short—in every detail of the bird's anatomy, physiology, and behavior. All of these features are, moreover, in continual interaction and dependent upon each other. For example, a bird has large flight muscles on its breast. The breastbone, correspondingly, becomes the largest bone in the body to support these muscles. The circulatory system is, in turn, built such that these muscles receive large amounts of blood during flight. The further you investigate, the more you come to see how every part is inextricably entwined with every other part. Goethe formulated this relation succinctly:

> All its parts have a direct effect on one another, a relationship to one another, thereby constantly renewing the circle of life; thus we are justified in considering every animal physiologically perfect. . . . Nothing can be added to one part without subtracting from another, and vice versa. (Miller, p. 121)

This wisdom-filled relation of the parts of an organism to each other is known in the science of comparative morphology as the law of compensation, or the law of the correlation of parts (after Cuvier).

It is one thing to establish the fact that organisms are fully integrated beings, it is another matter to understand in a concrete case how everything in an organism hangs together. A true science of the wholeness of organisms is still in its infancy because it puts new demands on our thinking capacity. Holistic thinking demands that we immerse ourselves in details and then move from detail to detail, but with an eye toward the whole organism that expresses itself in every part.

Some of my most rewarding moments of teaching occur when I succeed in taking this approach with students. Why? First, because we are involved in a process of real discovery. I tell the students that we're searching for an understanding of animals and plants that they won't find in textbooks. Together we may find relations that have not yet been discovered. Second, because when those moments of insight arise—Aha! I see how these two things are connected—they are deeply satisfying. We have touched something essential. The animal or plant has begun to reveal its deeper nature.

Let me give an example from the twelfth-grade zoology block. While amphibians (frogs, toads, newts, and salamanders) all lay their eggs in water, reptiles (lizards, snakes, turtles, and crocodiles) lay their eggs on land. This fundamental difference between these two groups of vertebrates is mirrored in their overall anatomy, physiology, and behavior. The eggs of amphibians are protected by a jellylike mass and float weightless in water. The growing embryos take oxygen out of the water and nourishment from the yolk-rich egg. In contrast, the eggs of reptiles are covered with a dry, papery-like shell (which is hard and calcified in crocodiles, like in birds). Within the shell the embryo floats in its own egg-made fluid within the so-called amniotic cavity. The protection and buoyancy the amphibian embryo receives from its watery environment, the reptile creates internally through an additional embryonic organ. Even when an animal like a reptile lays its eggs on land, its life begins in water—but in its own self-produced amniotic fluid.

The comparatively isolated reptile egg, resting in sand, soil, or leaves, has another "problem" compared to amphibians: in the amphibian embryo, gases and waste products diffuse in and through the medium of the surrounding water. The reptile compensates for this loss of connection to its immediate surroundings by creating an additional internal organ—the allantois. This blood-rich organ functions as an embryonic lung as well as a bladder that collects urine.

The more immediate relation of amphibians to a watery environment extends into their further development. Amphibians go through a fishlike stage as larvae (tadpoles). They breathe through gills and swim limbless, propelled by a tail fin. They then experience a striking metamorphosis into adults. They lose their gills and develop lungs, limbs develop, and, in the case of toads and frogs, the tail is completely reabsorbed. Only after this metamorphosis can an amphibian leave its natal pond and venture onto land. (Some amphibians remain their whole lives in water.)

Amphibians have moist and permeable skin. In fact, they breathe more through their skin than they do through their lungs. The skin lets not only gases in and out, but also moisture. For this reason amphibians remain bound to a moist environment even if, as is the case with many frogs and toads, they spend most of their adult lives out of water. When subject to dry air, a frog or toad will lose large amounts of its body moisture content. When it comes into contact with water again, the body quickly replenishes fluid loss by drawing water in through its skin (osmosis). A dehydrated frog need not drink with its mouth, it can just stick a foot in water and suck up all the water it needs!

Every year in spring the amphibian's strong relation to water comes into play when the adult returns to the pond where its life began. The female lays its eggs that are immediately fertilized—the water once again acting as a medium—by the male's sperm.

Just as the amphibian's connection to water shows itself in its anatomy, physiology, and behavior, so does the reptile's origin in a self-contained egg on land find expression in its other characteristics. In contrast to the amphibian, the reptile hatches from its egg as a small version of the adult. It already has a thick, cornified, and dry skin. The skin is virtually water-impermeable. Just as the reptile egg becomes independent from an external watery environment, carrying its own fluid, so does the adult reptile's skin allow it to detach itself from the need for direct and ongoing contact to water. For this reason reptiles can live in very arid climates by conserving body fluids for long periods of time and producing very concentrated urine to minimize water loss. Their whole physiology is built around the independence from water.

Of course, many reptiles are water-dwelling—marine turtles, crocodiles and alligators, water snakes, and so on. They nonetheless lay their eggs on land and have thick, impermeable skins. In this way they are primary land creatures that then seek the water after hatching. Through their skin they remain in a sense detached from water within water, unlike amphibians.

The reptile's skin is not only impermeable to water but also to gases. Correspondingly, its lungs develop more pockets and a greater surface area to take in the inhaled air. Lung development is always correlated with the development of the circulatory system. In reptiles the heart has four chambers through which arterial and venous blood coming from the lungs on the one hand, and the rest of the body on the other, remains completely (in crocodiles) or mostly (in other reptiles) separate. In contrast, amphibians have three-chambered hearts in which the blood coming from the lungs and from the rest of the body is mixed together. Again we see the quality of interpenetration in amphibians, and increasing separation and differentiation of internal organs in reptiles.

Through such considerations, the students see how each group of animals is a unified whole. They see how the amphibian's life and structure are imbued with an intimate and open relation to water, not only in general terms but in all details of reproductive behavior, embryonic development, skin, breathing, and circulation. The reptile has closed itself off from the immediate interdependency with the watery world, and every facet of its being speaks of this separation and the corresponding development of inner functions and structures. The understanding of each group is heightened by the contrast to the other. This is why I often work with comparisons, so that the unique features of each animal stand out much more distinctly.

To come to this kind of understanding demands that we not only register the characteristics, but that we actively re-create them in our imaginations. We need to form a saturated inner picture of, say, the amphibian embryo floating in water, surrounded by a clear jelly that mediates the exchange of substances and gases through the water. When we have built up this picture and then consider the amphibian's skin—thin, moist, and permeable—we see the same quality in another characteristic. This is holistic thinking.

Holistic thinking is so difficult because in our society we learn on the one hand to hold facts at a distance and on the other hand to use our imaginations in making pictures that have no relation to the external world. We don't bring the two together. Coleridge distinguished between fancy, which involves arbitrary picture making, and true imagination, which engages the world. In holistic thinking we need true imagination. We enter into a given phenomenon with our active imaginations and form pictures, we move to the next feature and build a new picture. In this sustained, wakeful process the wholeness of the creature can light up. This light can then illuminate further characteristics as one deepens the study of organism.

The wonderful thing about this process is that otherwise isolated details become interesting, because they help shed more light on the organism as a whole. For example, only when I'd begun to grasp the underlying difference between amphibians and reptiles did the way they make poisons begin to speak, that is, to tell me something about the animals themselves. There are very poisonous tropical frogs that secrete their poisons through glands that are distributed over their whole skin. When you pick them up and have a small wound on the hand, the poison can get into your blood and poison you. In contrast, the reptiles have poison glands concentrated in the roof of the mouth and must actively bite you and penetrate your skin with their fangs, through which the poison is injected into you. Isn't this the same contrast we have seen before, but now showing a new nuance?

To my mind, one of the most important tasks of Waldorf education is to reach this level of understanding in the eleventh and twelfth grades. It is not for nothing that in developing the curriculum with the teachers of the first Waldorf school, Steiner suggested that many of the twelfth-grade main lesson blocks have the character of an overview. We can build on the knowledge gained in previous years and pull it together to see overriding trends—in history, the evolution of consciousness; in chemistry, the different kinds of substances and transformations that characterize the different kingdoms of nature; in biology, the overview of the major phyla and classes of plants and animals. And so on.

Nothing is more important than to help the students school their abilities to see relations and connections, to see how things fit together in the world. This is precisely the capacity humanity needs to find creative solutions to the myriad problems we create that lead to a dissolution, rather than to a building-up of the world.

ACKNOWLEDGEMENTS

The Rudolf Steiner School is grateful for the generous support of those

who made possible this anniversary edition of *Educating as an Art*:

THE RUDOLF STEINER FOUNDATION

RENATE AND ARTHUR SOYBEL

ERICA AND JERRY TRACHTENBERG

BIBLIOGRAPHY

BIBLIOGRAPHY (PART 1)

Dennis, John. *Structural Geology.* New York: The Ronald Press Company, 1972.

Lyell, Charles. *Principles of Geology.* Vol. 1. Chicago: University of Chicago Press, 1990. (This book was originally published in 1830 and is a classic in geological literature; it contains a wealth of examples, including the Serapis Temple.)

Rauthe, Wilhelm. "Steps in the Development of Thinking." *Waldorf Science Newsletter* 3, no. 4 (1996): 8–12.

Steiner, Rudolf. *Education for Adolescents.* Hudson, N.Y.: Anthroposophic Press, 1996. (Lectures held in 1921.)

BIBLIOGRAPHY (PART 2)

Bulloch, William. *The History of Bacteriology.* 1939. Reprint, New York: Dover, 1979.

Coleridge, Samuel Taylor. *Biographia Literaria.* London: J.M. Dent & Sons Ltd., 1975. (Coleridge wrote these essays between 1800 and 1817.)

Darwin, Charles. *The Origin of Species.* 1859. Reprint, London: Penguin Books, 1979.

Evans, Alfred. "Pettenkofer Revisited." *Yale Journal of Biology and Medicine* 36 (1973): 161–76.

Goethe, Johann Wolfgang von. *Scientific Studies.* Edited by Douglas Miller. Princeton: Princeton University Press, 1995.

Holdrege, Craig. "Skunk Cabbage." *In Context* 4 (fall 2000): 12–18.

——— "Addressing Contemporary Issues in the High School: The Example of Human Cloning." *Renewal* (fall/winter 2000): 28–31.

——— "Where Do Organisms End?" *In Context* 3 (spring 2000): 14–16.

——— "Seeing Things Right-side Up: The Implications of Kurt Goldstein's Holism." *In Context* 2 (fall/winter 1999): 14–19.

——— "Science as Process or Dogma? The Case of the Peppered Moth." *Elemente der Naturwissenschaft* 70 (1999): 39–51. (A shortened version of this article appeared as "The Case of the Peppered Moth Illusion" in Whole Earth, spring 1999.)

————"Genes and Life: The Need for Qualitative Understanding." *In Context* 1 (spring/summer 1999): 11–15; and in *Waldorf Research Institute Bulletin*, June 1999.

————"The Sloth: A Study in Wholeness." *Society for the Evolution of Science Newsletter* 14 (winter 1998): 1–26.

————"Seeing the Animal Whole: The Example of Horse and Lion." In *Goethe's Way of Science*, edited by D. Seamon and A. Zajonc. Albany: SUNY Press, 1998, 213–32.

————"The Cow: Organism or Bioreactor?" *Orion*, winter 1997, 28–32.

————*Genetics and the Manipulation of Life: The Forgotten Factor of Context.* Hudson, N.Y.: Lindisfarne Press, 1996.

Howard-Jones, Norman. "Robert Koch and the Cholera Vibrio: A Centenary." *British Journal of Medicine* 288 (1984): 379–81.

Knight, David. *Robert Koch.* New York: Franklin Watts, 1961.

Lechevalier, Hubert, and Morris Solotorovsky. *Three Centuries of Microbiology.* New York: Dover, 1974.

Ogawa, Mariko. "Uneasy Bedfellows: Science and Politics in the Refutation of Koch's Bacterial Theory of Cholera." *Bulletin of the History of Medicine* 74 (2000): 671–707.

Rauthe, Wilhelm. "Steps in the Development of Thinking." *Waldorf Science Newsletter* 3, no.4 (1996): 8–12.

Schad, Wolfgang. *Die Vorgeburtlichkeit des Menschen.* Stuttgart: Verlag Urachhaus, 1982.

Steiner, Rudolf. *Faculty Meetings with Rudolf Steiner.* Vols. I and II. Hudson, N.Y.: Anthroposophic Press, 1998. (These meetings were held between 1919 and 1924.)

———— *Education for Adolescents.* Hudson, N.Y.: Anthroposophic Press, 1996. (Lectures held in 1921.)

Wieninger, Karl. *Max von Pettenkofer.* Munich: Heinrich Hugendubel Verlag, 1987.